GW00578968

This is the authorized story of my
career, written by a man who knew me when I
first started and who has been with me
ever since.

James J Braddock
World's Heavyweight Champion

RELIEF to ROYALTY
The Story of
JAMES J.
BRADDOCK

WORLD'S HEAVYWEIGHT CHAMPION

by LUD
Sports Editor, Hudson Dispatch
Union City, New Jersey

Foreword by
DAMON RUNYON

With two photographs and nineteen
illustrations by the author

DEDICATED
TO
HADDON IVINS
WHO GAVE ME MY
CHANCE TO DRAW
AND WRITE

To Damon Runyon, who wrote the foreword, to Jackie Farrell, who helped evolve the book's title, to Abe Zecker, who furnished sound advice on the printing problems, to the members of the sports staff of the Hudson Dispatch who helped in gathering and assembling the material, and to my ever-encouraging wife, Josephine, who typed the various drafts and who always proved a source of inspiration, I wish to extend my thanks.

THE AUTHOR

Contents

Foreword

IN ALL the history of the boxing game you find no human interest story to compare with the life narrative of James J. Braddock, heavyweight champion of the world.

Before Braddock came along, if any writer had offered, in fiction form, to any magazine, or to the scenario departments of the movies, the set of circumstances that befell Braddock, the tale would have been dismissed as wholly improbable.

Fiction and movie editors like their stories to be about something that could happen. This couldn't have happened—before Braddock came along. I don't want to sound trite, but believe an old plot-maker, truth in Braddock's case is much stranger than fiction.

Before Braddock, I had three favorite life stories of heavyweight champions. One was the story of dapper James J. Corbett, who stepped out of a clerk's cage in a bank to box his way to the title. Another was the story of mighty Jack Dempsey, who dropped from a hobo's precarious perch on the brake beams, to slug his way to the crown.

The third, and to me, best of all, was the story of James J. Tunney, who worked seven long years to strengthen his hands, and to fill out his body before he reached the top, then retired, married a wealthy society girl, and now lives the life of a Connecticut country gentleman.

But James J. Braddock has made these stories seem pale and uneventful.

Mark you, Braddock was contemporaneous with both Dempsey and Tunney, but through the years of their greatest pugilistic glory, he attracted only passing attention. Only one man that I know of ever made bold to suggest that Braddock might one day occupy the chair of the pugilistic king, and that man was Joe Gould, Jim's voluble manager.

1

I remember Braddock as a mere stripling fighting preliminaries, with Gould hanging onto the lapel of every sportswriter he could catch, babbling of Braddock's future. That was around the mid-Twenties, and as the Twenties faded into the Thirties, Braddock's future seemed to be going with them.

By 1933, he was regarded as "washed up," and he vanished completely from the pugilistic news of the day. You heard rumors that he was working as a laborer on the docks over in New Jersey, then that he was on public relief, for Jim had a wife and children, and he couldn't let them starve.

You didn't see much of Joe Gould in those days, but when you did, and you asked him about Braddock, he invariably said that Jim was all right, and that he'd be back some day, and he always said it with a courage that quelled any possible doubt in your mind as to Joe's sincerity. But you didn't believe it—that Braddock was ever coming back.

Then in June of 1934, Braddock was offered a couple of hundred dollars to fight one Corn Griffin, an ex-soldier from Georgia, and it is my conjecture that Jim was expected to be a stepping stone in the advancement of Corn. It was a preliminary to the Baer-Carnera title fight, and the circumstance of Braddock getting off the floor to knock out Griffin passed almost unnoticed in the excitement of the main event.

But that night hope was born anew in Braddock's heart.

He always could punch. He found he hadn't lost his punch. He realized that he still could fight, and he felt that his Destiny, lost for many weary months, had finally found its way back to him.

The night he won the title by defeating the garrulous, flashy Max Baer, I referred to Braddock as "The Cinderella Man," for truly, here in real life, was the old story re-enacted in its elementals with a big pugilist in the leading role.

I happened to be one of the few who contended from the beginning that Braddock was entitled to the match with the champion, and after the match was made, insisted that Jim had a chance to win.

But I confess now that the night of the fight, in the face of the overwhelming public opinion against Braddock's chances, and the betting odds of 1 to 10 in favor of Baer, I commenced to weaken on my own judgment.

No contender for a title ever entered the ring conceded so little chance. Braddock, as he stood up to be introduced, was regarded by many of the ringsiders as a pathetic figure, as merely a pugilistic sacrifice to the glory of Baer.

Only little Joe Gould, again, seemed cock-sure and confident as he stood proudly beside big Jim—that is, only Joe and Braddock. They had come a long way over a rough road together to this night.

And so Braddock won the big title, and in the time he has held it, he has endeared himself to the American pugilistic public by his unchanging modesty, his affability, and his sturdy character. His devotion to his wife and family, his capacity for "mixing," and withal his attitude as champion of the world that he will fight anybody regardless of color, or creed, has made him the most popular champion in the history of the game.

He is a great fellow, and he has a great story, and it is a privilege and a pleasure to me to introduce it with this foreword.

DAMON RUNYON

Preface

WHEN James J. Braddock, of North Bergen, New Jersey, won the heavyweight championship of the world from Max Baer on the night of June 13th, 1935, the general reaction in most quarters to what was described as "the greatest fistic upset since the defeat of John L. Sullivan by Jim Corbett," was that the Jerseyite was the luckiest man ever to have ascended the heavyweight throne.

James J. Braddock was lucky TO HAVE OBTAINED A SHOT AT THE CHAMPIONSHIP. But those who said he was the luckiest man to win the championship were neither fair nor accurate.

They forgot, for instance, that in 1930 Max Schmeling, of Germany, won the heavyweight championship of the world while he was lying on his back in the ring of the Yankee Stadium ; they forgot that Schmeling and Sharkey never would have been fighting for the championship that night had not Gene Tunney vacated the throne two years before; they forgot that two years later in 1932, when Sharkey was declared the winner on points over Schmeling and thus was crowned the new champion, that he finished the fight in such miserable condition that the newspaper boys are still arguing that Schmeling won and should never have been deprived of his crown; they forgot, among other things, that when Jack Johnson, the only Negro heavyweight champion, licked Jim Jeffries to finally attain legitimate recognition as the title-holder in 1910 that the Jim Jeffries whom he knocked out that blistering Fourth of July day in Reno, Nevada, had not had a fight in EIGHT LONG YEARS when he crawled through the ropes; they forgot that when this same Jeffries was crowned champion himself in 1899 that the Bob Fitzsimmons whom he stopped was a pugilistically old and decrepit individual of 36 years; they forgot that Jess Willard, the Pottawatomie Giant, when he succeeded Jack Johnson as champion in 1915, had to go 26 rounds to win the title under the most peculiar circumstances at

Havana, Cuba—that Johnson's entire purse was not turned over to his wife at the ringside that day until after the 20th round, and that it was not until she signaled that she had collected the required moneys that Johnson finally rolled over at the appropriate moment and was counted out in the 26th round as he was shading his eyes from the sun.

Yes, all that was forgotten on the night of June 13th, 1935, when the family man from Jersey with the stout fighting heart and in absolutely the best condition of his life out-pointed in 15 rounds at Long Island City the vaunted Max Baer from California—who had been hailed on all sides "as the greatest champion since Dempsey."

The author will concede that Braddock was fortunate to be designated as the challenger against Baer.

Only a combination of the most unparalleled circumstances, as outlined in the pages to follow, served to shove him into the challenger's seat that night.

But that he was lucky to win the championship . . . . .

LUD SHABAZIAN

Union City, New Jersey,
August, 1936.

Introduction

OF the great John L. Sullivan, first of our recognized Queensberry champions, the legends are many. It is said that one day, while he was out walking with his dog, he signaled a horse-car and made to board it.

But dogs were not allowed on trolleys in those days and the conductor (who, had he recognized Sullivan, surely would have forgotten all rules) kicked Sullivan's dog off the platform. Whereupon Sullivan kicked the conductor off.

On another occasion, in the very midst of one of his roaring drunks, he decided he was in desperate need of a haircut. He immediately set sail for his favorite barbershop only to find when he entered that sacred American institution that another customer was in *the* chair. Bellowing with rage at what he considered the most insolent effrontery, he bashed his fist squarely into the lathered face of the innocent but nonetheless offending customer and then heaved the poor unfortunate out of the place.

Some time afterwards, while touring, he declared he was being "persecuted" by the police of Philadelphia, for "causing a crowd to gather." He allowed one such incident to go by without an eruption, but when, the next day, another copper began to annoy him on a similar account, John L. cut loose. He clutched the offending minion of the law by the nape of the neck and whirled him under one arm. Then, despite the copper's screams and squirms, he headed for the nearest water fountain (some four blocks away) and there gave his molester a royal dousing that that worthy must have remembered to the very end of his days.

But there was only one John L. Sullivan.

Half a century—a span of fifty years—has rolled by since the "Boston Strong Boy" was in his heyday. Over a dozen heavyweights have ascended to the -throne from which he thundered. Some great fighters—the Corbetts and Fitzsimmons and Jeffries and Dempseys and Tunneys followed in John L.'s wake—but none of them, least of all James J. Braddock, around whose circuitous route to the championship this book revolves, resembled john L. Sullivan in manners and modes, both in the prize ring and out.

There has not been a fighter since who could bellow and blast and then back up his words like the great John L. James J. Corbett, who succeeded Sullivan, was a suave, slick, polished teller out of a San Francisco bank. Bob Fitzsimmons, one of the real marvels of the ring, was one of its most gallant characters as well. Jack Johnson was an egotistical playboy. So was Max Baer. Jess Willard was a big, good-natured giant, hardly fitted for the role into which he was thrust in April, 1915. Primo Carnera was cast in a similar mould. Jack Dempsey was a restless raging, driving volatile force, always on the go, hardly able even to sit still. Tunney was studious—and more often than not, aloof and haughty. Max Schmeling, the German, was a shrewd, stolid type, who kept a good deal to himself, and Jack Sharkey, the Boston Gob, was something that at times literally bordered on the hysterical.

INTRODUCTION

Of the fourteen glove champions who preceded him, Jim Jeffries is the only one to whom Braddock may be compared—and then in a very peculiar respect. Corbett once said of Jeffries that he had never seen a man who had "so little aptitude for boxing." Loughran said the identical thing about James J. Braddock after whipping him in a bout for the world's light-heavyweight championship in 1929. But both Jeffries and Braddock later became world's champions.

There, however, the comparison ends. There can be absolutely no comparing of their records. For while Jim Jeffries rammed his way to the world's heavyweight championship in his tenth professional fight, Braddock drifted about the sea of professional pugilism for ten long years before he was crowned the titleholder.

His is a remarkable story.

Let us start at the beginning.

CHAPTER ONE

THE BIRTH OF A CHAMPION

IT IS the year of our Lord 1906.

The great Jim Jeffries, like the mighty Alexander, has looked around and finding no more worlds to conquer, has resigned as world's heavyweight champion.

Striving desperately to gain recognition as his successor are a number of second-flight heavyweights—Marvin Hart, Jack Root and Tommy Burns. But already looming menacingly in the offing is the huge figure of a dusky stevedore from Galveston, a Jack Johnson, whom destiny has marked as Jeffries' successor.

Joe Walcott is generally recognized as the boss of the welterweights. In the division just above, a terror from Grand Rapids is elbowing his way madly to one spectacular knockout after another. His name is Stanley Ketchel. The world's lightweight champion is none other than that will-o'-the-wisp from Baltimore—the great Joe Gans, and shouting lustily for a crack at his crown is Oscar Matthew (Battling) Nelson. The man who is to bring them together a few months later and who in two more decades is to become known as the world's greatest promoter—is smoking cigars and prospecting gold in the Nevada mine fields. His name is Tex Rickard.

Boxing is enjoying a glorious era. True enough, Terry McGovern and George Dixon have neared the end of their careers. But fellows like Mike and Jack Twin Sullivan, Willie Lewis, Jack Blackburn, Jimmy Britt, Young Otto, Johnny Coulon, Jim Flynn, Young Erne, the Dixie Kid, Leach Cross, Packey McFarland, Joe Jennette, Sam McVey, Iron Hague, and a dozen others are making great reputations for themselves.

In the midst of this period of distinguished fighting men, a notable event occurs on the morning of June 7th, 1906, in the small New York City flat of the Braddock family at 551 West 48th Street—only a couple of blocks away from the site, where, 20 years later, a new Madison Square Garden is to arise.

For on that morning, another child, a bulky 17-pound son, who is to be named James Walter, and who is some day to win the world's heavyweight championship, is born to sturdy Joseph Braddock, and his charming wife, Elizabeth O'Toole Braddock.

Elizabeth O'Toole Braddock, mother of the new-born babe, first saw the light of day in Manchester, England. She came of Irish parents. Her mother, Mary Oates, was born in Galway, in the province of Connaught, while her father, Thomas O'Toole, was a native of Sligo, in the same province.

Also from Connaught came her husband's mother, a Julia Reddington. But Julia Reddington's husband, whose name was Jim Braddock, and after whom the new child was named, was born in Cheshire, England, and established the English strain in the family.

Although the new babe's father and mother had been born within ten miles of one another in "the old country" (Joseph Braddock's birthplace was a little hamlet known as Mottrem, only ten miles from Manchester), they did not meet one another until they had emigrated to the United States. "Elizabeth came to America first, in 1887. Joseph Braddock landed about two years later, crossing the ocean, incidentally, on the same vessel which brought Jake Kilrain over for his memorable 75-round fight with John L. Sullivan at Richburg, Mississippi. Charley Mitchell, also famous as a Sullivan opponent, and who was to act as Kilrain's second in that fight, was aboard ship, too.

Some years after arriving in America and settling in the colorful West Forties of New York City, a section which had none too euphemistically been nicknamed "Hell's Kitchen," Joseph Braddock met and became enamored of Elizabeth O'Toole. The romance flowered and when he finally had mustered up enough courage, Joseph Braddock proposed to Elizabeth. He was accepted, and in due time they were wed.

Seven children blessed the union, six of whom were born in New York City. In the order of their arrival upon this planet, the children were Nellie, Julia, Ralph, Joe, Jack, James Walter, and Alfred.

Nine weeks after James Walter was born, his parents showing scant consideration for the new arrival's desires in the matter, moved from the West Forties of New York City across the Hudson River to New Jersey, and settled in the peaceful township of West New York, which nestled atop the Palisades. Pa Braddock now had quite a brood to take care of, with half a dozen children around the house. But the trucking and moving business which he started proved remunerative and he managed to make ends meet.

Following the distinctly novel pattern first established when Cain and Abel appeared on the face of this earth, the Braddock children grew up.

Like other boys, Jimmy Braddock played marbles. Like other boys, he played "three—ole-cat." Like other boys, he played baseball—and was an outfielder. Like other boys, he continued to play "shinny" long after twilight—and was regularly reprimanded for being late for supper. Like other boys, he loved to go down to the river and plunge in for a swim. Like other boys, he wanted to be a fireman or a locomotive engineer. Like other boys, he saved those small, brightly-colored pictures of prize fighters, ball players, warships and birds—then to be had with every purchase of cigarettes by their elders. Yes, and like other boys, he positively hated books.

He attended St. Joseph's Parochial School, in West New York, but admits somewhat ruefully that no medals were pinned on him. He "hated arithmetic like it was poison," and to this day shows a pronounced aversion to mathematical computations, even though thousands of dollars may be involved, leaving all such reprehensible labors to his manager, Joe Gould. He detested geography and had no burning affection for history, either—but his friend, Marty McGann, insists "Jimmy wasn't a bad speller."

According to McGann, the class "had a spelling bee one day and Jimmy was the only boy left standing. But they got him on a trick word and one of the girls won."

Mr. McGann was unable to recall the exact nature of the etymologic sorcery whereby our hero was eliminated from the competition.

It was with this same Marty McGann that Braddock, at the tender age of 11, and in the middle of winter in the bargain, decided to see the world. Having hatched their bold plan the night before, the would-be globe-girdlers, arising early took an extra helping of pancakes from the table, stuffed them into a bag and the while virtuously informed their mothers that "some extra lessons" would keep them at school during noon hour and that they would not be back until after the afternoon session.

But no more than school was let out at noon than the wanderlust-bitten chums tramped down the hill to the railroad yards at the West Shore Ferry. Taking the necessary precautions to avoid detection, they slipped quietly into a New York, Ontario & Western box car—and then sat back to await developments.

They had not long to wait.

A long, heavy rumble and the grinding of wheels soon informed them that their Big Trip Around the World had begun.

"I always wanted to see Chicago," elatedly exclaimed Jimmy.

"Aw, why stop at Chicago," said the more daring McGann. "Let's go to California first."

"That's right," replied jimmy. "We've got nothing else to do. We might as well. Say," he remarked in high glee, "think of the kids back in school, eh."

"Yeh, I am thinking of 'em," his companion replied. "They'd enjoy this trip."

Slowly, the huge freight lumbered out of New Jersey and headed for upstate New York. Off and on, the youngsters peeked outside, saw the snow-laden countryside, and then went back to their "bunk" in the car. By and by, however, an unpleasant but not at all strange sensation began to annoy them.

"I'm beginnin' to get hungry," said jimmy.

"So'm I," replied Marty.

"And it's beginning to get dark, too," said jimmy.

"Well, we can't get off this train while it's movin'," said the very elemental Marty.

Things were just beginning to approach a state bordering on deep gloom when the freight, slowing down, finally came to a stop. Our heroes at once jumped off the train. They soon learned that their Big Trip Around the World had carried them as far as Washingtonville, New York.

Something besides darkness and hunger now overtook the explorers. They found themselves shivering from the cold.

"It was so cold, we had to keep running to keep warm," explains Jimmy. "While we were bouncing around, the freight started to go again. We yelled to one another and headed again for the train."

"But by the time we got to the caboose, we had been noticed and all our efforts to hitch on were in vain. We were beaten off by a trainman with a lantern."

"We were up against it now. Far away, in the now almost complete darkness, we spied a light. There was only one thing to do and we did it. We headed for the light and finally came upon a farmhouse. We knocked on the door. A woman opened it, saw us, screamed, and then slammed the door shut again. A moment later, a man opened the door. He had a shotgun in his hand."

"We were scared, but managed somehow to get our story across. He agreed to put us up for the night if we would chop him some wood the next day. Of course, we agreed at once, and after giving us something to eat, and asking us where we were from and everything else, he put us to sleep."

Our heroes slept late the next morning, very late. While they were slumbering away, the farmer got in touch with the authorities, who in turn notified the worried parents in West New York. The news came from West New York that someone would arrive on the eleven o'clock train the next morning to take the culprits back. The farmer returned home, roused the sleeping boys, and put them to work. They were weary indeed when they went to bed that night.

The next morning, the farmer hustled the boys over to the depot, and chuckling to himself, awaited the eleven o'clock train.

In time, the train pulled in and two sorely tried Irish paters disembarked therefrom to look for their errant offspring.

The fathers Braddock and McGann minced no words when they got within exploding distance; neither did they spare the palm. The ride back home was a rueful one and a considerable portion of it was spent in a standing position, for that particular part of their anatomy on which the boys usually sat had been fanned—and fanned plenty.

Sheepishly, Jimmy Braddock returned to school the next morning. Then, for the next three or four years, he conducted a sporadic attack on the three R's. But books continued to remain undesirable quantities to young Jimmy Braddock, who was more at home at the edge of the old swimmin' hole on the Hudson River, or beneath the bridge on the Hackensack River.

He didn't get much "book—larnin" but he did manage to pick up considerable practical experience in the use of his fists, with which he was later to earn his livelihood.

They wrote of John L. Sullivan that, when a boy at school, he rarely had fights with the other boys because both sides knew before the fight began that Sullivan was the better man. This, however, was not true of Jim Braddock. Our hero had fights and many of them, and there were many occasions when the other fellow finished "the better man."

"There were about 35 boys in my class," he once explained, "and they could all fight a bit. We were always busy," he concluded significantly.

Jimmy's most formidable opponent seems to have been a lad named Jimmy Morris. Braddock and Morris tangled something like 30 times, with honors even. McGann, who acted as Braddock's second in all these fights (by holding Braddock's coat) kept track of the victories and defeats. "Jimmy would win once, but in the very next fight, Morris would have the edge. I don't think any one of them ever won two in a row," he positively announces, recalling the shindigs.

Also in Jimmy's class was a lad named Elmer Furlong, who, however, was not destined to be as fortunate as Jimmy Morris in holding his own. Furlong was the first kayo victim of Jimmy Braddock's pugilistic career. Jimmy's reaction to the terrific punch with which he levelled Furlong, however, was anything but pleasant.

In one of those schoolboy arguments that start with a marble game, the Furlong boy, one day went to it with Braddock. A savage mixup soon had all the kids from the corner looking on pop-eyed. Suddenly, Braddock landed a terrific right, flush on Furlong's chin. His pal dropped as though he had been felled by an axe. His head hit the concrete walk— and as he lay there unconscious, one of the onlookers yelled:

"Elmer is dead!"

Hot and cold shivers ran alternately up and down Braddock's spine. When, finally, a doctor had to be called to attend the still unconscious and stretched out Furlong, our hero began to have the most horrible visions. But after half an hour, Furlong recovered consciousness and Braddock heaved a sigh of relief. He still recalls, however, the miserable half hour he spent that afternoon in the schoolyard while Furlong was stretched on the concrete.

CHAPTER TWO

HIS FIRST FIGHT IN A RING

A FEW months after the Furlong knockout, Jimmy Braddock decided that he and school were not properly mated and that a separation would be highly desirable. Of course, this decision on his part occasioned a bit of unpleasantness around the family table, but our hero's mind was made up and in due time he left the halls of St. Joseph's without benefit of a diploma.

His first job was as a messenger boy for the Western Union and he delivered wires through most of 1919. On the Fourth of July of that year, he was heading for West New York with a batch of telegrams in his hat when he passed the offices of the *Hudson Dispatch*, a morning newspaper published in Union City, and saw a huge crowd congregated outside the building. Our hero forgot at once about the telegrams.

From a second-story window that day, the *Hudson Dispatch* was megaphoning a round-by-round description of a struggle for the world's heavyweight championship between Jess Willard, of Pottawatomie, Kansas, and Jack Dempsey, of Manassa, Colorado. Radio broadcasts were unknown then and Haddon Ivins, editor of the *Hudson Dispatch*, had decided that interest in the fight warranted a megaphone announcement.

Thousands turned out to hear the blow-by-blow account of the annihilation of big Willard by Dempsey at Toledo—and among the thousands in front of the Dispatch Building was a skinny, open-mouthed young man in the uniform of a messenger boy, who excitedly drank in the bulletins that were being announced by Vic Lane (now assistant sports editor of the *Hudson Dispatch*) and Bill Bengal, a printer.

Little did the messenger boy of July, 1919, dream that sixteen years afterwards, he was to whip Max Baer, a protégé of Jack Dempsey's, to win the championship that Dempsey himself was annexing under a broiling Toledo sun that afternoon.

As a matter of fact, Jimmy at that time never even thought of boxing as a means of livelihood. Such thoughts were not to enter his mind until a few years later.

After several more months of delivering telegrams, he became a printer's devil. Then a teamster. Then an errand boy in a silk mill.

Then, one fine day, the wanderlust bit him again. Accompanied by several pals, he decided to ride the rails. This time, he got further than Washingtonville—this time, he hoboed as far west as Chicago.

Weeks later, he returned home.

After he had stowed away his first respectable meal in months, he picked up one of brother Joe's sweaters, pulled it on, and headed for Nurge's Field, nearby, to see "the gang."

An hour or so later, Joe Braddock got home himself.

Around this time, Joe was quite some pumpkins of a fighter. He had fought his way through the amateurs until he had won the New Jersey State Amateur welterweight championship, after which he had turned professional under the guidance of a grinning and jovial Irishman named Barney Doyle, who in those days could have spotted Dumb Dan Morgan seven hundred verbs and pronouns and still held his own with the Orator of 49th street.

The first thing Joe Braddock looked for when he returned from work was his sweater.

"Jimmy took it," said Ma Braddock.

"Oh, he did, eh," rumbled Joe. "Then he's back."

"Yes," replied Ma Braddock. "He went over to Nurge's to see the boys."

Without saying a word and forgetting entirely about supper, Joe Braddock headed at once towards Nurge's Field to teach "that young upstart" a lesson. He would punish Jimmy not only for taking his sweater—but also for running away from home to Chicago.

The scrap that resulted when Joe Braddock and Jimmy Braddock squared off that day in Nurge's Field is still talked about in the northern part of Hudson County.

Joe was four years older than Jimmy, and also had rating as a professional pugilist. Jimmy, on the other hand, was a green, skinny kid.

Yes, Jimmy Braddock entered the fight with his brother the underdog, a role which though new then, was to be a common one for him in the years to come.

Accounts of the fight differ. The boys, it seems, fought a grueling struggle that lasted almost an hour and was a real throwback to the London prize ring days when men fought on turf and nothing was barred. They surged and battled all over Nurge's Field before someone hollered "cheez-it, the cops." Just who won is hard to say, for things were still progressing merrily when the end came. But all hands agreed that Jimmy Braddock surprised everybody—mostly brother Joe.

It was this fight that gave our hero the idea he might get somewhere in the ring.

About six weeks later, he fought his first ring battle under odd circumstances.

The event occurred at Moose Hall, Grantwood, N. J., on the night of November 27th, 1923.

Brother Joe, who "had not spoken to Jimmy since the row at Nurge's Field, was on a card at Moose Hall. Half an hour or so before the fight, he was lying down on a cot in a dressing room, waiting for his turn to be called to the ring, when Harry Buesser and Loz Fundarek, two of Jimmy's pals, suddenly appeared in the doorway.

"What's the matter now?" demanded Joe, sensing that the visit had something to do with Jimmy.

"Jim's got a chance to go on as a substitute in the last four-rounder," Buesser replied, "and he wants to know if he can use your trunks and shoes."

"Wait a minute," said Joe. "What name is he going to fight under?"

"He's not going to use his right name," said Fundarek. "He's going to fight -under the name oi Jimmy Ryan."

"All right, then," growled Joe, surrendering his fighting paraphernalia.

A few minutes later, Joe had pulled a pair of trousers on and along with Barney Doyle, had marched to the edge of the crowd to view the proceedings.

The fight that followed was Jimmy Braddock's first in a ring, and it must be recorded here (no doubt to the horror of New Jersey state's amateur authorities) that our hero thus fought as a professional long before he hammered his way to a collection of New Jersey State amateur championships. He got three dollars for his services.

And he lost the fight.

His opponent was Tommy Hummell, now a member of the Fort Lee, N. J., Police Department. Both Hummell and Braddock hit the deck several times before the finish. Newspapers the next day announced that Hummell had had an edge over his young rival. But they also agreed that the fight was the best one of the night.

Joe Braddock was quite pleased over his younger brother's performance against Tommy Hummell.

"All right," he finally announced after listening to Jimmy's pleas, "if you insist on fighting, you may join the Irish-American A. C., and start in the amateurs." This was a reversal of the usual procedure, but young Braddock wasn't worrying about procedure. So, with Brother Joe's blessing, Jimmy Ryan—the pro—was buried forever and Jimmy Braddock—Ryan's other half—became a chaste and undefiled simon pure, seeking worlds to conquer. It was a break for the Amateur Athletic Union.

Within a few months, both Joseph Braddock and Barney Doyle were convinced that they had in "the baby of the stable" a coming champion. Though the two mentors spent hour upon hour in a ring pitched in a cellar drilling the neophyte in the uses of a left hand, it was the explosive punch that he soon uncovered in his right hand that made them rave to the sportswriters.

"He just murders 'em with that right," Doyle would start with a grin on his face. Then would follow a dissertation that would last for hours while all present listened. Joseph Braddock, more or less a man unto himself, always permitted Barney to do all the talking. But he had no choice in the matter. Barney, who must have been born literally alongside the Blarney stone, would have resented even the slightest encroachment on his speaking rights.

But Barney and Joe both feared Jimmy would become a one-sided fighter. So, just before they shot the young gossoon into the amateurs, they called him aside one afternoon and delivered what they considered a very important lecture. Looking very sober, they advised Jimmy that, although he COULD knock 'em dead with his right hand any time he pleased, it would be considered bordering on the order of a very high intelligence for him to remember that he also had a left hand. Joe, who had learned from bitter experience, tried to be particularly emphatic about this.

Unfortunately, however, (or perhaps one should say "fortunately") Jimmy Braddock reverted to his left hand only when he found himself with his back to the wall. He discovered, after he got going, that it was so easy to knock opponents out with his right, that he just didn't have time to bother with his left. But he never forgot what had been drilled into him during those elementary sessions with young Freddie Huber, Joe Pepperted, Johnny Duff, and others in the Huber's cellar (headquarters for the New jersey Irish-American Athletic Club). And in some of the toughest spots of his career—when it would have verged upon suicide for him to gamble with his right, he fell back upon the smart use of his left hand to win fights—and a few championships.

Once Jim Braddock got started in the amateurs, he proved a terror. Doyle, always in the hair of sports editors, now began to appear on the other side of the rail more frequently than ever. What was more, he gave evidence of prosperity: he was now ALWAYS smoking cigars. "We just won another championship," he would start. Braddock's ordinary victories usually meant an effusion of some twenty minutes for Barney; but championships always meant a panegyric oration that lasted anywhere from an hour to two hours, with no words barred.

Braddock won medals and gold watches by the dozen. He fought as an amateur for something like two years, and in that time, rolled up 45 victories for the New Jersey Irish-American Athletic Club and a Chautauqua record for his manager. Of his 45 victories—no less than 30 were scored by knockouts. Every championship he won in the amateurs—he won by the same means—a knockout.

He won his first boxing championship on Saturday night, March 21st, 1925, and emulated the feat of the great Jack Dempsey in doing so. He knocked a man out with a punch to the jaw—and the punch not only stiffened his foe, but broke that unfortunate's ankle, too, just as Dempsey had broken Bill Brennan's ankle with a similar punch.

Johnny Emerson, out of Springfield, New Jersey, was Braddock's victim that March night at the National Turners Club in Newark. The prize was the light-heavyweight amateur championship of the State. Emerson lasted only one minute and 47 seconds.

Two nights later, Braddock threw brother Joseph and the now almost verbally exhausted Doyle into a frenzy as he won the state's heavyweight championship, too, even though he weighed only 161½ pounds!

Three men were drawn that night (March 23rd) to compete for the state's heavyweight title. Braddock, 161½ pounds, was one. Tom Burns, 209 pounds, was another. And Roy Bodman, 211 pounds, completed the list.

Bodman drew a bye in the first round and sat by and watched as the frail-looking Braddock went on against the 209-pound Burns. "He'll murder your man," remarked Bodman as Doyle marched by.

"He'll WHAT?" stormed Barney.

Only a few minutes later, Braddock had knocked Burns out with almost the first punch of the fight, a terrific left hook to the chin.

"You're next," said Doyle to Bodman.

Late that night, at 11:30 p. m., Braddock went on with the even heavier Bodman. A right to the jaw finished him in one minute and 57 seconds.

They gave Jimmy a beautiful watch in token of the championship. Doyle showed that watch to every sports editor in Northern New Jersey.

One year later, he again smashed his way to the state amateur light-heavyweight and heavyweight championships. This time, he won both titles in one night, February 28th, 1926. He won the light-heavyweight crown quite easily, but in the final for the heavyweight championship, he ran into a tough 215-pound stovemaker named Frank Zavita, out of Somerville, New Jersey, who gave him the fight that he still considers "the toughest battle of my career."

Braddock had put on every bit of half a pound in weight during the period from March, 1925, to February, 1926. So when he twisted his 162 pounds through the ropes to face the 215-pound Zavita that night at the National Turners, he looked almost anemic in comparison to his steel-muscled and burly foe from the central part of the state.

"Here is one guy he won't lick," murmured the crowd. Even though the fans had come to expect great things of Braddock—Zavita looked entirely too tough and too formidable. As if to confirm their judgment, Zavita, in the first few seconds of the fight, sank a left hook into our hero that all but tore Jimmy apart.

"Over ten years I've been in the ring," murmured Braddock some months after he had won the world's championship, "and in those ten years, I've been hit by some pretty stiff punchers. But," he concluded as he rubbed his side tenderly, "that punch Zavita smashed me with in the first round in Newark back in 1926 was the hardest punch I ever caught in my life. Why," he almost gasped, "I think I can feel it yet."

To add to Jimmy's discomfiture, Zavita, after booming that left into his 162-pound foe, snarled as he saw Braddock double up:

"What's the matter? Are you going to quit?"

As Zavita rushed in and began raining punches anew, Braddock found the building reeling around him. He was now sick in the stomach, and his heart was pumping like mad. He saw the blurred figure of Zavita, snarling and punching, and in this first agonizing and crucial test of his fistic career, instinct—and the lessons he had learned from brother Joe, saved him. He stuck out his left hand. And he kept sticking it out. And Zavita, plunging in like an enraged bull in an effort to end the bout hurriedly, ran pop-pop into these lefts.

Braddock doesn't know yet how he escaped being knocked out in that first round. "All I remember is sticking out my left and clinching when I had the chance," he says.

Joe Braddock and Barney Doyle worked feverishly over him in between the first and second rounds.

"Now when you get out there," hoarsely shouted Doyle into Braddock's ear, "keep your left in his face."

Braddock did. Zavita began to be annoyed. He just simply could not get past the left. He began to swing wildly with his right. And eventually he left an opening that Jimmy couldn't resist. With every bit of strength he could muster, Braddock drove a right at Zavita and the crowd went into a delirium as the huge boilermaker flew through the air and landed on the canvas.

But putting Zavita down and keeping him down were two different accomplishments. Zavita, roaring with the fury of a wounded lion, jumped to his feet and rushed at Jimmy again. It was what Braddock had been waiting for-almost praying for. As Zavita came in, Braddock whacked the left into his face, measured him and banged over with another bone-crushing right hand. Down to the deck hurtled Zavita again.

Believe it or not, before the fight finally ended with Braddock the winner by a knockout in the third round, Zavita had hit the canvas no less than eleven times all told. The fans, standing on their chairs, were yelling like mad at the finish.

They still talk about that fight in amateur circles in New Jersey. And whenever Braddock talks about it, he always insists it was the toughest fight of his career.

CHAPTER THREE

A PROFESSIONAL

WITH the Zavita fight over and the state's heavyweight and light-heavyweight championships his for the second year in succession, Jimmy Braddock decided that his record of thirty stinging knockouts in forty-five amateur fights warranted turning professional at last. This time, he fought under his right name and this time, his brother, Joseph, not only knew about it, but was his manager as well.

The story of how Joseph Braddock had decided that he and not Barney Doyle would handle Jim's pugilistic destinies started away back on the night of January 9th, 1925, even before Jimmy had won his first amateur championship.

On that particular night, Joseph Braddock, then in his second year as a professional, crawled through the ropes at Amsterdam Hall in old West Hoboken, New Jersey, to fight Andy Lake, his foremost local rival. Lake, a smart, two-fisted puncher, had been a sensation in the amateurs himself before turning pro. As a matter of fact, he had won the Jersey state welterweight crown in 1922, the year before Joe Braddock ascended to the same throne. And naturally, when Braddock, who lived only a few blocks away from Lake, won the title in 1923, talk of a fight between the two men quickly filled the air. It was not until after Joe Braddock had fought professionally for two years, however, that Barney Doyle consented to the match.

The northern part of Hudson County was wildly excited over that fight and a crowd of some fifteen hundred persons jammed its way into the stuffy hall to witness it. While the fighters were getting the instructions from the referee, Manager Doyle, who besides being an expert monologist was quite a psychologist, too, drew a chalk-line across the center of the ring, and then turned around to taunt Lake:

"Meet my man halfway," he said, "and we will knock your block off." Like all other fight managers, Mr. Doyle warmly relished the first-person plural when it came to inflicting damage on the other fellow.

Lake did meet Braddock halfway and for a spell in the first round, it seemed as though Braddock had knocked his opponent to Kingdom Come. He landed a terrific right beneath the heart that split Lake amidships and threw Manager Doyle into a frenzy.

But Braddock was over-cautious and failed to follow up his advantage. Lake managed to weather the storm of that one almost decisive punch. Nevertheless, it took two more rounds before his head cleared completely and in those two rounds, Joe Braddock piled up a big lead. But in the fourth round, a terrific right behind the ear, followed by a left to the stomach, sent Joe Braddock to the deck, unconscious.

So chagrined and so vexed was Barney Doyle when he saw his fighter counted out, that he whirled around and stalked away from Braddock's corner in the highest dudgeon.

Joe Braddock never forgave Doyle for deserting him.

He vowed that night, on his way home, that he would see to it that although Doyle was his manager by contract, the same Doyle never would be Jimmy's manager. "I'll manage him myself if he amounts to something," he said to himself.

In the next fifteen months, Jimmy Braddock did "amount to something," and when he finally turned professional on the night of April 14th, 1926, it was Joe Braddock who got him the fight.

Jimmy Braddock did not make his legitimate pro debut with a victory. He fought Al Settle at Amsterdam Hall in a four-round, no-decision affair that was tough going all the way for both Braddock and his colored opponent. At the finish, the bout was adjudged a draw by the newspapermen at the ringside.

But one week later, on April 22nd, at Ridgefield Park, N. J., Braddock went to town against George Deschner, a baker boy from Union City.

"I feinted him with a left in the second round," says Jimmy, "and boom!—the right hand finished him."

For those two fights, Jim got the lucrative sum of $50; $15 for the Settle affair and $35 for the Deschner kayo.

"You've got a few bucks now. Guess you had better train from now on at Joe Jennette's gymnasium," his brother told him. Jennette, veteran colored heavyweight, operated a gymnasium over his garage at 27th Street and Summit Avenue, in Union City. He also taught the youngsters a thing or two on the side—and Jimmy felt he could stand a few lessons.

So, possessed at last of money enough to pay the monthly fee and also to get himself a locker, young Braddock headed for Jennette's gymnasium.

The move turned out to be the most important of his career—for it was while he was training at Jennette's one afternoon in the spring of 1926 that he met Joe Gould.

CHAPTER FOUR

ENTER JOE GOULD

BELIEVE it or not, it cost Joe Gould just six hundred and fifty dollars to make the acquaintance of Jimmy Braddock.

Back in 1925-26, Gould, then a young fight manager, had under his wing a top-rank welterweight named Harry Galfund, who had knocked out, among others, fellows like Larry Estridge, Sammy Baker and Bobby Barrett. He was, however, a hard man to handle, and when, one fine day, a group of Hoboken beer barons offered to buy his contract, Gould readily agreed to sell.

A price of $2,500, which was to be divided evenly between fighter and manager, was set upon his head.

On a Wednesday afternoon in June, 1926, the interested parties appeared at Jennette's to close the deal. Galfund was to go through a workout before the money changed hands.

Gould looked around for somebody to throw in there with Galfund. There was only one person available. That one person was a stranger, a skinny-looking lad, who was over in a corner, punching the bag.

Gould walked over to the unknown.

"Say, do you want to make five dollars?" he asked.

The youngster nodded in the affirmative. Five dollars was a lot of money.

"All right," snapped Gould, "get in there and work two or three rounds with my man."

As the youngster got into the ring with Galfund, Gould began smoking a cigarette in the corner, and the Hoboken sportsmen, who had come prepared to pay $2,500 for Galfund' s contract, began to look on expectantly.

The story of that workout was to become history. Galfund rushed at the youngster but ran smack dab into a straight left that sent him reeling backwards.

Shaking off the effects of that unexpectedly stiff poke, and smiling to the onlookers as though it had been an accident, Galfund ran at the youngster again. But again, that left hand stopped him cold.

Gould threw away his cigarette and began to perspire a bit. The Hoboken sportsmen began to elevate their eyebrows. The youngster, instead of wilting, kept poking Galfund solidly with lefts, and, as his confidence increased, began to jar him occasionally with rights. Only at close quarters—where his weight and experience told, was Galfund able to score.

Gould was mad through and through. when the round finally ended.

"Go in there and kill him. What the hell are you trying to do—ruin the sale now?" he hissed at Galfund. "All right, Joe. I'll get him this round sure," grimly replied Galfund.

He is irritable when excited and very easily excited. He cocks his head to one side when angry and fixes a withering glare on those who annoy him. He has a sharp, resonant voice and yells so hard during a fight that he is often hoarse for days afterwards. He will jabber and chortle with glee when something pleases him. Yes, he does swagger, but he always backs it up. In his day he has made and spent a fortune managing fighters; however, he still enjoys life.

His passion is golf and most of his time is spent on the links, where he delights in wheedling newspapermen into small bets. He has a keen, raking memory and can remember what the elephant forgets. That's Joe Gould.

He is happily married and lives with his wife Betty just off Central Park, in New York City.

JOE GOULD, *Manager*

39

But the second round was no different from the first and the third round, which ended the proceedings, was even more annoying to Gould and Galfund. As the gong sounded, Gould felt certain the sale had been ruined. And he already had spent part of his end!

The Hoboken sportsmen, however, who had seen Galfund in some of his better performances were still insistent on buying—but not at the original price. They saw a chance to do some heavy chiseling. They offered a thousand dollars and after a little haggling, agreed on $1,200.

The money changed hands then and there (in those days it was not uncommon for Hoboken sportsmen to march around with forty or fifty one-hundred dollar bills in their pockets).

Gould lit another cigarette, counted $600 out for Galfund's end, turned it over to his ex-fighter, and then marched over to the lanky kid who had just cost him so much money.

"Here's ten bucks instead of the five I promised you," slick Joe began. "Have you got a manager?"

"No," came the answer, "my brother does my business."

"Do you know me?"

"You're Galfund's manager, Joe Gould, aren't you?"

"That's me," replied Gould. "When can I see your brother?"

"Well, he's a plumber—" started Braddock.

"Swell," said Gould, seeing a patch of daylight.

"But he's off Saturday afternoons and you can see him then," finished Braddock.

"Tell him I'll be here Saturday afternoon at two o'clock and you be here with him," directed Gould.

And on a Saturday afternoon in May, 1926, Joseph Braddock, the plumber, turned the pugilistic future of his younger brother, Jimmy Braddock, over to Joe Gould, a dapper and voluble manager from Cauliflower Alley.

And thus began a relationship that has been rarely paralleled in the fight game. When Gould and Braddock teamed up that Saturday in 1926, a two-year contract was drawn up between them. Joseph Braddock, who knew a little about such things, saw to that. But that contract ran out in 1928—and it was never renewed.

"There never was any necessity," explains Braddock.

But seven years later, in April, 1935, in the hectic days which preceded Jimmy Braddock's designation as the Number One Challenger for Max Baer's heavyweight title, the New York Boxing Commission insisted that the rule requiring fighters and managers to have contracts on file, be lived up to in this case, too.

So a new agreement was drawn up after all those years.

"How many years shall we make this contract for?" asked Gould.

"Oh, I don't care," facetiously replied Braddock. "Make it fifty or a hundred years. It's the same to me."

CHAPTER FIVE

JOE GOULD, MANAGER

THE Joe Gould whose name will appear frequently through the remaining pages of this book, was born on August 14th, 1896, in Poughkeepsie, N. Y., just a few miles away from Hyde Park, the birthplace of President Franklin Delano Roosevelt. He was the son of Ida and Benjamin Goldstein, whose right name was Benjamin Biegel, but who erroneously had been listed upon his arrival in this country as Benjamin Goldstein because the relatives who had greeted him at Ellis Island upon his arrival had been Goldsteins.

When the years rolled by and Pa Biegel became conversant enough with English to realize that an error had been made in his name, he decided that it was too late to ask for a correction which involved, among other things, a lot of red tape with the authorities. So the family name remained Goldstein. But Pa Biegel's fifth child, Joseph, who was to become associated with the fight racket, became known as Joe Gould when he invaded the celebrated caverns of Cauliflowerdorn. And Gould is now his legal name.

Joseph was the fifth of Pa Biegel's nine children. He was, also, the only son who showed a tendency to veer away from the professions.

Aaron, the eldest, became a lawyer. Irving went to the University of Pennsylvania and became an eye doctor. Harvey studied, too, for a spell but later decided to enter business and is now associated with Joe. Rose, the first daughter, became a school teacher. Sarah, who followed Joe into this world, became a school teacher, too. Sam studied law and became a magistrate in Newark. Edith, not to be out-done by her sisters, also was a normal school graduate, and Charles, the last son, went in for accounting.

Perhaps the fact that he became associated, early in his childhood, with quite a few individuals who were to figure prominently in boxing later on in their lives, had something to do with Joe Gould's reluctance to follow the fond desires of his father and take up a profession. When little Joe was but a tot of two years, the family left Poughkeepsie and moved to New York City, taking up residence there at 49 East 112th Street. In the same building there lived a family known as the Leiners, and the Leiners had a son named Benjamin. A block away, on 113th Street, lived the Lippmans, and the Lippmans had a tall, lanky offspring whose name was Robert.

Benjamin Leiner and Robert Lippman were two of Joe Gould's earliest and closest pals. In the years to come, the Leiner boy was to fight his way to the world's lightweight championship under the *nomme de guerre* of Benny Leonard and to be recognized as one of the greatest lightweights of all time. And the Lippman boy was to become Leonard's trainer and later Gene Tunney's trainer and still later, James J. Braddock's trainer—under the nickname of "Doc" Robb, a handle which was to be fastened upon him by Billy Gibson, Leonard's manager.

When young Joe Gould reached high school age, the family moved again—this time to Jersey City. There, in the teeming downtown section where Coles Street crosses Third, young Gould grew up along with Morris Barison, who was later to become a judge, Jack North, who was to gain fame as an actor, and Sam Cohen, Eddie (Ryan) Aufseher, and the Diamond brothers, Lew and Sammy, who were to become identified with boxing in various capacities.

Joe Gould's first real job was as an "apple butcher" on the Erie Railroad trains, running between Jersey City and Haverstraw. But he soon decided that there was no future in that and elected to enlist in the navy. Sammy Diamond joined with him.

"They put us on an oil tanker," explained Gould, "and that's where I learned to smooze those matchmakers and promoters into giving my fighters good spots."

Before long, however, young Gould decided that his chances of becoming an admiral were not bright either. He confided as much to Diamond—and was surprised to find that Diamond felt likewise. Eventually, they emerged from the service.

Around this particular time, Gould's lanky pal, Sam Cohen, was pulling down a fat salary working as a meat inspector in the slaughterhouses along the Jersey City waterfront. Gould's father, anxious to see his son settle down, continued to plead almost daily with Joe to take a fling at the Civil Service tests for inspectors. And during these pleas, he invariably pointed to Sam Cohen as a sterling example of a young man with gumption who had taken the tests, passed them and was now going places.

More to please his father than anything else, Joe Gould finally went to Trenton one day for the examinations. When the marks were put up, however, Joe not only was far from the head of the class, but actually had failed to make even a passing mark. His paper showed only 65 percent. A strange fate, however, contrived to make a meat inspector out of Gould, despite this low percentage. For only a year or so after he took the test, America became engulfed in the World War and the experienced meat inspectors were drafted for the military. This created a shortage of inspectors in civilian ranks and so it came about that one fine day, Joe Gould was notified that he had a job.

"Just imagine," he chuckles as he recalls the incident, "I got $65 a week as an inspector—and what I didn't know about meat would have filled a whole stockyard."

His stroke of good fortune, however, failed to last very long. Germany soon capitulated to the Allies, an Armistice was signed, and the war was over. The regular inspectors came back to work and before the year was out, Joe Gould was looking for something else to do.

This time, he finally found his niche. He became interested in managing fighters and Lew Diamond, who had just piloted Johnny Buff, a Jersey City flyweight, to two championships (and who is now a boxing promoter in Tampa, Atlanta, New Orleans, and other southern cities) was his mentor.

The handling of fighters turned out to be right down Gould's alley. He clung to this new activity assiduously and by 1925 he had become a more or less prominent figure in the racket. He and the late Pete Stone, known more familiarly as Pete the Goat, were partners for a long spell. They formed a good combination. Pete was the silent half of the partnership. He was a strong-armed individual who had a baleful gleam in his eye, who could whip boxers into shape, and who was, for more reasons than one, a positive influence in a corner. Gould, on the other hand, a younger man, very dapper and not at all abashed under any circumstances, did the "fronting," the outside business and almost all if not all the talking for the firm. He was the spender of that partnership, too. Pete the Goat let very little slip through his fingers. When he died some six or seven years later, he left a fortune reported to run into six figures. At the time his former partner was stone broke, despite the fact that he had at some time or other in his career managed such fighters as Italian Jack Herman, Harry Galfund, johnny Reisler, Frank Carbone, Pal Silvers, Dave Shade, Ray Miller, Kid Francis, Nat Pincus, johnny Pincus, Young Zaccone, and perhaps a dozen others besides James J. Braddock.

CHAPTER SIX

BEGINNING OF A PARTNERSHIP

AS A LIGHT HEAVY-WEIGHT...

IT WAS in June, 1926, that Jimmy Braddock fought his first bout under the management of Joe Gould.

Only a few days after Joe Braddock had entrusted Jimmy to his care, Gould ran into Charley Doessereck, who had just become matchmaker for Boyle's Thirty Acres. The huge pine bowl at Thirty Acres, in which Jack Dempsey and Georges Carpentier had drawn the first million-dollar gate five years before, was piling up a big tax bill for Tex Rickard. In an effort to "get off the nut," Tex had agreed to let Doessereck run a series of popular-priced shows there.

Doessereck signed Tiger Flowers and Young Bob Fitzsimmons to top his first show and was busy whipping together a preliminary card when Gould buttonholed him.

"I've got a young Jersey heavyweight . . ." began Gould.

"I know him," said Doessereck to Gould's surprise. "I've seen him fight in the amateurs; he's pretty good. Tell you what I'll do. I'll put him in with Leo Dobson. You'll get $75 for the fight."

Doessereck wasn't giving anything away, however. Braddock was a bid card in Jersey.

The match closed; Gould called Braddock up to sputter the good news.

On the afternoon of June 18th, 1926, the fighters showed up at Thirty Acres to weigh in. Braddock was on hand early, but there was no sign of Dobson. "Where is this fellow we're going to fight?" asked Gould of Doessereck. "We want to get a look at him."

They waited around for half an hour and then another half hour, but Dobson failed to put in an appearance. Meanwhile, Braddock stepped on the scales. He weighed only 163 pounds.

"You're sure this Dobson is a light-heavyweight?" asked Gould.

"Yes, yes," assured Doessereck. "Don't worry about him. He'll probably be around early tonight to weigh in."

Braddock was not at all worried, but Gould, who knew the tricks of the fight game, was beginning to get just a bit suspicious. His suspicions were confirmed early that evening. Shortly after seven o'clock, he and Braddock appeared at Thirty Acres and made for the dressing room. As they wended their way beneath the pine boards, Gould nervously cast his eyes about looking for "this fellow Dobson." Suddenly he ran into Hughie Gartland, well known manager and handler from Newark. Gartland had a fighter on the card, too.

"You've got somebody on?" asked Gartland.

"Yeh, a new fellow I've just picked up—Jim Braddock," Gould replied.

"Who's he fighting?"

"A guy named Dobson."

Gartland whistled.

"Can your guy fight?" he asked.

Gould looked at him.

"I'll tell you why," explained Gartland. "This fellow you're fighting has won 14 straight fights by knockouts."

Gould reeled. His head began to whirl. And as he groped about in a half-daze, Dobson appeared on the scene and jumped on the scales. He tipped the beam at 189 pounds! Gould all but collapsed.

Suddenly Gould decided that he had been tricked and that under no circumstances would he permit Braddock to go into the ring with a fellow who had 26 pounds weight on him. Marching over to the dressing room, he ordered Braddock to get back into his street clothes.

"We are not going to fight any guy weighing 189 pounds," he roared.

But he ran into unexpected opposition from Braddock.

"Don't worry about the weight," protested Jimmy. "I'm used to fighting guys who outweigh me. Didn't I fight that Frank Zavita who weighed 215 pounds to my 162? Besides," added Jimmy, "I need the money. And all my friends from North Bergen are outside—waiting to see me fight."

Gould, however, perhaps more concerned over Dobson's 14 straight knockouts than the fact that he weighed 189 pounds, was adamant.

"Nothing doing," he repeated over and over again. "We won't fight."

But finally, Jimmy prevailed upon his manager to permit him to go on. Before Gould capitulated, however, he singled out Charley

Doessereck and delivered a withering blast that made Charley's hair stand on end.

A few minutes past nine o'clock Jimmy Braddock crawled through the ropes. The size of the crowd had added to Gould's worries. How would Braddock, used to fighting before crowds of only several hundred persons in the amateurs, perform before this immense throng?

Gould's worries ended quickly, however. Despite the fact that Braddock was fighting before thousands of persons for the first time, despite the fact that his opponent had a weight advantage of 26 pounds on him, Jimmy Braddock stepped out and knocked Leo Dobson out in the second round to the delirious delight of hundreds of his admirers from North Bergen itself who had turned out to see him in action. The first round was a cautious one but in the second Braddock marched after Dobson in earnest. Two slashing lefts blasted their way into Dobson's stomach. Another booming portside hook to the same place finally lowered Dobson's guard and through the opening thus created, Braddock flung a pulverizing right that put Dobson down and out.

It was in this fight, his first for Joe Gould, that he became known as "James J." Braddock. At the time of the Dobson fight, Jim Jeffries, the ex-champion, and Tom Sharkey, his pal, were doing a vaudeville bit in and around New York City. Gould met big Jeff on Broadway one day and the accidental meeting gave him an idea.

A few nights later at Thirty Acres when Announcer Jack Merity asked the name of his fighter, he was ready.

"It ain't Jimmy Braddock anymore," he replied. "It's James J. Braddock."

So as James J. Braddock he was introduced. The name clung to him through the rest of his career.

James J. Braddock mounted the fistic ladder rapidly, thanks to the careful, or shall we say "adroit," match-making of Joe Gould. By the end of 1926 he had scored fifteen victories, twelve of them by knockouts. He stopped, among others, fellows like Johnny Alberts, Walter Westman (whose ribs he broke), Jim Pearson (who was managed by the famous old lightweight Joe Shugrue), Gene Travers and Carmine Caggiano.

Soon, Jess McMahon, matchmaker at Madison Square Garden, heard of the young Jersey puncher, and began to make overtures for his services. Gould, however, took his time about signing to fight in the House that Tex Rickard had built. He was not sure in his own mind as yet whether Braddock was ready for a shot in the Garden.

But finally, he decided the time was ripe and early in the winter of 1926-27 young Braddock fought for the first time in the ring in which he was later to attain nationwide fame. He met George LaRocco, of New Rochelle, a splendidly put-together youngster who had won 28 fights himself and who was being hailed on all sides as one of the best prospects in the game.

Braddock, however, made short work of LaRocco. He knocked the New Rochelle puncher out in the very first round and threw not only Gould, but all of Madison Square Garden into a deafening uproar. LaRocco's handlers at once clamored for a return bout. The return tussle was staged a few weeks later and ended in a draw. Then a third bout was arranged, and this time Braddock won by decision.

Things did not run smoothly in all of his fights, however. True enough, at the end of 1927 he had engaged in 33 fights all told, of which he had won 27 clearly, 16 of them by knockouts. But twice he was held even, and in several of the no-decision bouts which he fought in New Jersey, the newspaper consensus generally agreed that he had finished second best.

He did defeat, during 1927, tough fellows like Jimmy Francis, Nick Fadil, Vic McLoughlin and Jack Stone. He remembers that Stone fight at the West New York Playgrounds very well, for in the second round he was sent sprawling to the canvas for one of the very few knockdowns of his career. While he was down, taking a count of three, a young miss seated at the ringside became horror-stricken. But Jimmy got off the canvas and came on to beat Jack Stone, and the young miss at the ringside who had been so frightened, later on became his wife.

That bout, incidentally, was his first ten round fight.

Sixteen days later, on May 27th, 1927, at Arcola Park, New Jersey, not very far from his home town, he met clever Paul Cavalier, of Paterson. Not only was Cavalier an experienced fighter with a great left hand much too seasoned for Braddock—but in addition, the Paterson puncher out-weighed James J. by 14 pounds!—the figures being 176 to 162. Such a handicap was entirely too much for young Braddock—all the more so because the fight was over the ten-round distance.

Nonetheless, for two rounds, Braddock held his own with Cavalier, and in the third round smashed the Patersonian on the jaw with a right that sent Paul reeling across the ring and almost out. It was destined, however, to be his only real punch of the fight, for Cavalier saw to it that no more came over. The Paterson puncher either got in close where weight and experience told and where Braddock's right could get no momentum for any damaging punches, or he stayed away and stabbed his left repeatedly into Braddock's face. When it was over, there was some disagreement at the ringside as to who had won (as there always will be when a puncher meets a boxer) but Abe Green and Al Del Greco, sports editors from the Paterson and Hackensack newspapers, agreed that Cavalier had the edge.

Just twelve days later, on June 8th, 1927, while the Cavalier fight was still stinging his memory, Braddock fought the first of his three memorable fights with Jimmy Francis, of Union City—fights which are still discussed in his home county of Hudson.

They were Jimmy's first big "money" fights. He got close to a thousand dollars for his end in each rumpus. The shindigs were staged at the old West New York Playgrounds and when Braddock and Francis crawled through the ropes for the first one, almost seven thousand persons were looking on. The crowd was the biggest to fill the park since Tommy Loughran and Mike McTigue had fought there in 1923.

"Now this guy is a right-hand puncher," Gould explained before the fight began, "and he will rush you continually. You've got to do to him what Cavalier did to you a couple of weeks ago. You've got to keep circling away from his right and you've got to poke him steadily with your left hand as you do."

Braddock was soon to agree that Joe "spoke wisdom"—to quote Joe himself.

The gong sounded and Braddock, left hand extended, awaited Francis' rush. But Francis, under instructions from shrewd Doc Bagley, who had been imported as one of Francis' seconds for this very special occasion, did no rushing. With the result that the first round was very tame.

But shortly after the second began, the men were fiddling away in mid-ring when Francis suddenly leaped in and threw the Playgrounds into a frenzy with a terrific, vicious right to Braddock's jaw. For an instant, Braddock reeled. But instead of going down—as Francis, and all those who had seen the punch land had expected—Braddock suddenly became a raging madman.

Then, for the rest of that round and the next five rounds as well—right up to the eighth, the crowd which had flooded the park witnessed one of the wildest fights Hudson County had ever seen. The rugged Francis, possessed of a murderous right, seemed far more powerful than his slender, albeit taller foe—but Braddock simply astounded everybody by taking all of Francis' punches and fighting savagely back.

While Francis aimed strictly for the jaw and missed quite often—Braddock made everything count. When the opportunity offered, he riddled the body. And through those burning early sessions, Gould, in the corner, howled continually for Jimmy to "keep punching him in the body!"

In the fifth round, Francis slipped to the canvas but was up instantly. In the seventh round, after a wild rush and a scuffle, both fighters went to the mat together.

When the seventh round ended, the edge was with Francis. So far, he had been the stronger of the two and had landed the harder punches. Braddock had done some damage, too, but a good deal of the time he had been forced to hold Francis.

But in the eighth, ninth and tenth rounds, the tide swung sharply Braddock's way. Francis tired. Braddock, in splendid condition, began to grow stronger. Sensing that he would now be able to fight as he wanted—Braddock switched tactics. He began to box at long range, to flood Francis' face with jabs and to uppercut whenever Francis, crouching, waded in close. At the end of the ninth round, the fight had become more or less even and Braddock by winning the tenth round by a good margin, managed to eke out a margin of victory, slight though it was.

It was one of the toughest fights of Braddock's career, and he will tell you so to this day. Despite the fact that there had been no knockout, the seven thousand who had witnessed the scuffle buzzed loudly for days. So loudly that promoter Bill Hermenau and his matchmakers, Sam Cohen and Willie Weiss, got the men to sign for a return match.

The return match took place five weeks later, on July 13th, 1927. Both men weighed 168 pounds. In sharp contrast to the first affair, it lacked sparkle and fire. Braddock, now even in better shape than he had been before, smothered Francis, who at times actually appeared drunk, with long, left jabs. By the ninth round, Francis' cause had become hopeless. The Union City puncher waddled out to the middle of the ring and there uttered the celebrated dictum, "Come on and fight," generally hurled by all fighters who find themselves similarly shackled. Braddock, himself, was to say the same thing to Tommy Loughran a few years later. And just as Loughran—that night in 1929—replied by splashing a whole basket of left hands into his face—so on this occasion, did Jimmy sprinkle his left tantalizingly in Francis' face.

The second fight really settled the question of supremacy between Braddock and Francis, but they met once more, the following year, and Braddock won again—this time even more decisively.

The year 1927 also saw Braddock hook up with Joe Monte—a fighter whom he will remember to the end of his days. For Monte not only held him to a draw and not only gave him his "tin ear"—but also furnished the skull against which Braddock first broke his right hand.

During the year, Braddock had fought Hermany Germany Heller a tough ten-rounder despite the fact that he had a broken collarbone. But a broken hand was something else. Notwithstanding the severe pain over the third knuckle, Braddock went through several fights after suffering the break on Monte before he and Gould finally called upon the late Dr. William G. Fralick, an expert on damaged hands.

Fralick shook his head as he looked at the X-rays.

"You should have come here earlier," he reproached fighter and manager. "Now it will have to be rebroken and reset all over again and it will cost you one thousand dollars."

He might as well have said it would cost a million. Jimmy's fights so far had netted him a nice living, but no more. And Gould, despite the size of his fistic stable, spent so freely that a thousand dollars was a dim and distant sum to him, too.

So Jimmy just kept on fighting. Despite the condition of his mitt, he stepped out and knocked Jack Darnell out in four rounds, after which he swept into action against Paul Swiderski.

Here, one of those uncanny occurrences of Fate which were to stud his career took place. The very first right-hand punch which he fired at

Swiderski landed with such terrific force on Swiderski's head that it broke the hand again. Despite the pain, Braddock went through the remaining nine rounds and Swiderski, so stunned by that first punch, proved an easy decision victim, even though Braddock had to fight with only one hand the rest of the way.

Having rebroken the hand himself, Jimmy now permitted the doctors to reset it correctly. This time, it healed properly.

CHAPTER SEVEN

POINTING TOWARDS LOUGHRAN

WILLIAM
MULDOON

BRADDOCK floundered about a good bit during the early part of 1928. He scored his third victory over Jimmy Francis in the early part of the outdoor season but ran into considerable trouble after that fight.

On June 27th, he met Billy Vidabeck (now a policeman in Bayonne) at the West New York Playgrounds, and Vidabeck, a tall, strong, blond-haired chap with a boom-like left hand, gave him a headache. On July 25th, he fought Nando Tassi, the Italian, over the 10-round distance, and was held to a draw. And when, on the night of August 8th, Joe Sekyra pumped out a ten-round decision over him, the outlook became positively gloomy.

On what he had done so far, Braddock hardly deserved even ordinary mention.

As a matter of fact, he actually seemed to be slipping when Gould signed him for a fight which was to mark the first big turning point in his career.

The fight took place on the night of October 17th, 1928, at the Newark Armory.

Braddock's opponent was Pete Latzo, out of the Pennsylvania coal mines, a former welterweight champion, and a rattling good fighter. Latzo had been matched to fight a terror who was coming out of the West at the time—Tuffy Griffiths—for Madison Square Garden. As a tune-up for the Griffiths thing, he took on Braddock in Newark.

The bout made history. Braddock went into the ring conceded not a chance. Latzo ruled a five to one favorite. Yet before the evening was over, Braddock had not only defeated Latzo, but punched the former world's champion so severely around the head that Latzo's jaw was fractured in four places!

For three rounds, Latzo had a big edge on his slender but taller rival. He left-handed Braddock easily and seemed to be coasting to an easy victory when suddenly Braddock's right hand broke with a stunning impact against his jaw. Latzo never realized how badly he had been hurt. It was not until after the fight that doctors, examining the defeated fighter, found his jaw had been shattered so.

Courageously, Latzo fought on and on that night. In the ninth round, the Armory swam before his eyes as Braddock, punching murderously drove home three devastating uppercuts that nearly set him down each time. Through it all, however, Pete staggered and then clung on through the tenth, too, to avoid a knockout. Braddock weighed 173 for that fight, Latzo, 171.

Doctors had to use some eleven feet of fine wire to put Latzo's jaw together after the fight, according to Howard "Poke" Freeman, of the *Newark Evening News*. Not only that, but the courageous ex-champion had to be fed liquids for months and had to cancel fights which would have paid him some $25,000 in the next year or so.

Madison Square Garden made the only logical move under the circumstances. The man who had knocked Latzo out of the Griffiths shot was given the shot instead. So almost out of nowhere, James J. Braddock stepped into a headliner's position to fight Tuffy Griffiths at Madison Square Garden on the night of November 30th, 1928.

That memorable night, Braddock broke the hearts of both Tex Rickard and his rotund matchmaker, Tom McArdle, by taking on and knocking out in less than two rounds, a rip-snorting, smashing, devastating terror who had come roaring out of the West with a record of 54 consecutive victories and who was expected, at Braddock's expense, to make a whirlwind debut in Madison Square Garden. The Westerner's name was Gerald Ambrose (Tuffy) Griffiths—and to this day, fight fans recall the consternation which Braddock spread by toppling Griffiths four times before the fight finally was halted.

Oddly enough, when Tuffy arrived in New York several days before the fight, he decided to work at Stillman's gym where Braddock himself was training. Before Jim's very eyes, Griffiths, in two drills, flattened four sparring partners and the fans just about stampeded to watch him. Off in a corner, Braddock toiled in complete solitude. In view of the circumstances, this was only natural.

While Braddock had been flubbing around most of the summer of 1928—Tuffy Griffiths had been sweeping through the Midwest like a cyclone. Not in years had a fighter with such potentialities been uncovered in the corn-country.

No wonder Tom McArdle, one of the canniest match-makers in the country reached out and plucked Tuffy for an appearance at the Garden! On the night of August 22nd, at Chicago, Griffiths had flattened Tony

Marullo, a pretty tough fighter, in one round. Five days later, on August 27th, in the same city, he had whipped K. O. White to a frazzle in ten rounds. One month later, again in Chicago, he had met and knocked out in one round—none other than Mike McTigue, a former world's light-heavyweight champion!

Nor did he stop there. As the pugilistic world watched him with bated breath, Griffiths swept around the Midwest like a cyclone, flattening Joe Anderson in Detroit on November 9th in four rounds, blotting out Jim Mahoney, in Sioux City, Iowa, on November 13th, in three rounds and then cannonading Jackie Williams, at Davenport, Iowa, on November 22nd in one round!

He had a streak of four consecutive knockouts when he rolled into Madison Square Garden on the night of November 30th to a wild fanfare and acclaim such as few fighters ever had been tendered. The odds against poor Braddock ran as high as seven to one, and only one newspaperman, it seems, Marty Berg, of the *Bronx Home News*, had the temerity to say in the face of mass opinion the other way, that Braddock might explode the Griffiths bubble.

The Garden was jammed with 19,000 fight-mad fans that night. The whole town had turned out, it seemed, to see the lad who had been dubbed the second Dempsey. Braddock, all hands felt, was merely playing the role of the sacrificial lamb.

Griffiths scorned Braddock completely when the instructions were being given. Had he known that only a week before the fight Braddock had injured an ankle in training and that Joe Gould had been on the verge of postponing the match or calling it off, his confidence in himself might have been even greater. For a week, Doc Robb had worked desperately on that ankle, but finally, it had to be taped and encased in a special supporter for the fight.

As the bell sounded, Griffiths came sweeping out of his corner in a crouch and plunged right into the erect Braddock, both arms flying. Nothing could have suited Braddock better. The Jerseyite stuck out a solid left hand and Griffiths was sent back on his heels. But Tuffy was a strong young man. He snorted, and getting in close, started a whirlwind attack that almost swept Jimmy off his feet. Braddock, however, did not go down as most of Tuffy's past foes had. He weathered the storm and in the midst of the thundering tumult that was cascading from one side of the Garden to the other, ripped across a stream of left hands that stopped Tuffy in his tracks time and again.

Between the first and second rounds, Madison Square Garden buzzed with the wildest excitement. But the general feeling was that although the Jersey youngster had very cleverly lasted that first round, he never would survive the second.

As the bell sounded, Griffiths rushed across the ring, arms flying furiously again. Braddock began to time those rushes and the round was something less than one minute old when hell broke loose.

Braddock exploded a right hand on the westerner's jaw with every pound of his 171½ pounds behind the blow.

As 19,000 fans leaped to their feet, Griffiths stiffened, and then toppled to the canvas. In the midst of pandemonium, Griffiths rolled over. So groggy and dazed was he that instead of taking the count of nine, he staggered to his feet at three.

Braddock was oblivious to everything now. He was oblivious to his lame ankle. He was oblivious to the wild screams of the crowd. He was oblivious to the hysterical pleas of his seconds. All he sensed in the midst of that deafening uproar was that he had Tuffy Griffiths—the great Tuffy Griffiths—swimming before him, and that he must finish him. He cocked the old right hand, timed it perfectly again, and exploded it once more against Tuffy's jaw. Once again Griffiths went pell-mell to the canvas. The Garden rocked with excitement. Griffiths, still rubber-legged and glassy-eyed, now staggered up at "four."

No one who saw that fight ever will deny that Tuffy Griffiths had heart. In the midst of a din that shook the Garden to its very foundations, Griffiths rolled around the ring like a drunken sailor, his arms by his side, absolutely helpless, while Braddock leaped close and fired a steady, ceaseless, withering bombardment at his chin. No one on earth could have withstood such fire for long. Soon Griffiths sagged to the canvas again—for the third time in the round. Still game and still willing, however, he tried to rise at three, while a frenzied and sympathetic crowd implored hoarsely for him to take nine.

Though the mind was willing, however, Tuffy's flesh was weak. He fell again, this time before Braddock could hit him and here Referee McPartland stepped in and humanely stopped the slaughter. The round had lasted but one minute and forty seconds in all. Braddock had weighed 171½ to 173½ for Griffiths.

Immediately after the most amazing upset of the year had been scored, Tex Rickard, quick to take advantage of such situations, announced that he would throw James J. Braddock against Leo Lomski, the Aberdeen Assassin—the winner to fight Loughran in the summer of 1929 for the world's light-heavyweight championship.

A few days after the Griffiths fight, an incident which was to be recalled often in later years, took place. Ordered to appear before Boxing Commissioner William Muldoon, Gould and his fighter marched into the commission offices wondering what was in the wind.

Muldoon pointed a stern finger at Gould.

"Young man," he said, "I am going to hold you accountable for the development of this fighter. I saw him knock Griffiths out the other night and I enjoyed the fight. With a little weight on him, I predict he will someday win the world's heavyweight championship. But he must not be rushed along too rapidly."

With that, the 83-year-old Muldoon grasped Braddock's hand and shook it vigorously.

That prophecy never was forgotten by Jim Braddock and Joe Gould. Seven years rolled by, and William Muldoon was resting forever in a wind-swept grave at Tarrytown, N. Y., when Braddock defeated Baer in 1935 and won the championship to make the "Solid Man's" prediction come true. But it did come true.

Nor was Muldoon the only one to be tremendously impressed in 1928 by Braddock. A retiring heavyweight champion made an almost similar prophecy concerning Jersey Jim around the same time. Gene Tunney, who had stepped down from the heavyweight throne, declared in a newspaper article one day shortly after his retirement that it would not surprise him at all "were Braddock someday to win the heavyweight title."

Braddock was to experience many reverses, however, before the predictions concerning him were realized.

Six weeks after the Griffiths fight, on January 18th, 1929, James J. Braddock, now squarely in the thick of the light-heavyweight picture, slid through the ropes at Madison Square Garden to fight Leo Lomski. The fight proved a keen disappointment from the Braddock viewpoint.

For ten rounds, he and Lomski fought the sloppiest kind of a fight. When it finally ended, the judges disagreed—and Referee Arthur Donovan cast the deciding ballot in favor of Lomski. It is only fair to say that ringside opinion was with the referee, for a newspaper consensus showed six rounds for Lomski, three for Braddock, and one even.

Oddly enough, Braddock inflicted more damage than did Lomski that night. The Jerseyite caught his rival with a whirling right in the opening round and for a spell, the 17,000 fans who had paid over $60,000 to witness the milling, were yelling madly for a quick knockout. But Braddock failed to follow up his advantage. He was terribly slow. He shuffled around and hesitated, and in general muffed so many golden opportunities, that he aggravated even his warmest admirers. In the third round, however, he managed to get another right over. This not only staggered the westerner, but opened as well, an ugly looking gash on Lomski's left eyebrow.

Yet to the utter dismay of his followers, Braddock again allowed Lomski to escape. Steadily, the blood trickled from the cut over Leo's eye. But Braddock couldn't untangle himself to do any more damage. Eventually Lomski's head cleared a bit. The westerner sensed that another smash on the eye—and he might perhaps become the victim of a technical knockout at Braddock's hands. There was only one thing to do: stand off and jab, or whirl in close to prevent Braddock from getting any leverage for his right-hand swings. Perfect tactics.

Through the rest of the fight, Braddock swung and swung and swung that right—but all in vain. Lomski's left just dominated the picture. And as the rounds rolled by, weariness overcame Braddock, too. He was a very tired young man at the finish.

There was, however, some explanation for his poor showing and weariness that night. The fact that he had had less than five minutes of actual ring combat in three months (all against Tuffy Griffiths) had told as the fight wore on. No wonder he looked slow and awkward.

Braddock weighed 172 to 172½ for his conqueror.

But though his showing against Lomski had been quite unsatisfactory, Braddock did not eliminate himself entirely as one of the prospective challengers for Tommy Loughran's title. He bounced back quickly after the Lomski thing to stop George Gemas in just one round at Newark, and then on the night of March 11th, 1929, astounded the fans and critics as well by knocking out Jimmy Slattery, the Buffalo Adonis, in the ninth round of a scheduled fifteen round fight.

Close to 16,000 persons had bustled into Madison Square Garden to see the struggle between the two Irish Jimmies, who, along with Lomski, were the leading contenders for Tommy Loughran's crown. Slattery, who had been knocked out only twice in his career (once by Paul Berlenbach and once by Dave Shade) entered the ring an 8 to 5 favorite.

He was a brilliant boxer, a flitting will-o'-the-wisp, who, when he was good, was (like the little girl with the curl) very, very good.

For seven rounds, the clever Slattery eluded the continually charging Braddock. For seven rounds, Braddock chased the elusive foe before him, tagging him now and then, but never solidly. For seven rounds, the "flitting, flicking, dancing ghost from Buffalo" as Edward J. Neil, of the *Associated Press*, described Slattery, outsmarted and outboxed his slower foe.

But in the fading moments of the eighth round, one terrific right-hand smash turned the tide of battle and started the dancing Slattery on his way to doom. Braddock had just driven Slattery into a corner. Slattery tried to glide away. But Braddock had him figured for once, and starting a right hand from away back, he broke it with stunning force on Slattery's jaw. Badly hurt, Slattery fell into a clinch and was hanging on for dear life when the bell sounded.

They worked feverishly over Slattery during the rest period. Out he came for the ninth round, but those who were close to the ring realized that he was still dazed from the terrific wallop he had absorbed in the round before.

Braddock was quick to take advantage against Slattery. The mistakes of the Lomski fight were not repeated. Before Slattery (who always did carry his hands dangling by his side as he pranced around opponents, depending on speed more than blocking to get him away from punches) could get a guard up, Braddock had landed two punches and driven him reeling to the ropes. Here, Fate stepped in to help Braddock, too. Had Slattery been able to fall and take a count, he might have been able to avoid a knockout—for the time being, anyway. But the ropes kept him from falling back—and Braddock's frenzied punches kept him from falling forward!

In the midst of a deafening tumult, the Buffalo boy finally sagged and slipped sideways to the canvas. He was a pitiful sight. At five, he tried to get to his feet, only to fall back limply into the arms of Referee Lou Magnolia, who waved Braddock away and sensibly stopped the slaughter.

The ninth round lasted only one minute and twelve seconds. Braddock became the talk of New York after that knockout. The lone disputant now to his right to fight Loughran for the championship was Leo Lomski, who had pushed out a victory over him in January. And while Tom McArdle, the Garden matchmaker, was pondering the advisability of putting Braddock and Lomski against one another once again—pleasant news came from Philadelphia late on the night of March 18th.

On that night, Maxie Rosenbloom defeated Leo Lomski over the ten-round distance. And then, to completely prick the Assassin's bubble, Tuffy Griffiths, who had been knocked out by Braddock only a few months before, stepped up and handed Lomski another beating in Chicago only ten days later!

There was no alternative now for chubby Tom McArdle. James J. Braddock stood in bold relief as the outstanding challenger for the world's light-heavyweight championship.

Even Jimmy Braddock grins—a bit ruefully, of course,—when he thinks of his fight with Tommy Loughran. He trained faithfully enough for the clash with the champion. Saratoga Lake, chosen by Joe Gould for the preparatory siege, was considered one of the finest conditioning places in America. On various occasions, Jack Dempsey, Gene Tunney, Mike McTigue, Pancho Villa and a horde of others had trained at the spot, first introduced to the cauliflower trade by Dumb Dan Morgan, who, according to Wilbur Wood, of the New York *Evening Sun*, had taken Frank Moran, Jack Britton and K.O. Brown up there in 1915 "because the place was so lonesome at night that the fighters were only too glad to listen to Morgan talk to them for hours, just to keep awake."

Braddock arrived at camp on the 26th of June. He was given the same cottage in which Dempsey had slept some years before. The bungalow was about two miles up the road from Tom Luther's Sulphur Springs Hotel.

After a week or so of roadwork, boxing was added to the challenger's program. His sparring partners were by no means stumblebums of the variety usually seen at training camps. Gould had hired out Allentown Joe Gans, Red Boyette, Joe Barlow, Jack Hanlon and Jimmy's younger brother, Al, for sparmates and they worked vigorously with Braddock every day.

From the Fourth of July on, Braddock showed a steady improvement in form as he lashed and tore his mates apart. He scored knockdown-s almost daily—and the newspapermen covering his camp could not help but enthuse over his form.

Braddock seemed to reach his peak on the Saturday before the fight—in view of subsequent events, a little too soon. On that day, the author, who was alternating between Braddock's Saratoga camp, and Loughran's Hoosick Falls setup not very many miles away, thought Braddock was in superb condition. Joe Gould thought likewise, and remarked "Braddock seems on edge right now."

The next day, the author visited Loughran's camp—and Tommy looked dismal. He was swathed in sweaters and full-length tights as he worked, plain indication that he was still struggling to shed weight. He had been having trouble for over a year making the 175-pound light-heavyweight limit and some doubt actually existed as to whether he would be able to get down to the required weight for the fight.

The author drifted back to Saratoga on Monday and though Braddock continued to show terrific punching power, he seemed to have slowed down in other respects. He did knock Barlow out of the ring and Boyette and Gans both were floored, but in his finishing workouts on Monday and Tuesday, the challenger felt a steady tattoo of left hands beat on his face.

Something else was ailing him, too. He lost weight steadily from Monday on.

He had weighed 173 on Monday. On Tuesday he tipped the beam at 172½. Then, to the utter amazement of both Gould and Robb, he stepped upon the scales at the commission offices on the afternoon of the fight, and registered only 170 pounds! Between Monday and Thursday, he had lost three and one-half pounds.

Yes, something was palpably wrong with Jimmy. He had not slept well for days; he reflected it in his nervousness—and that nervousness was to be patently noticeable when he crawled through the ropes a few hours later.

Had the newspapermen known Braddock's exact condition, had they known before Thursday afternoon, for instance, that he was going to weigh only 170 pounds, and that he would enter the ring drawn entirely too fine, they might not have shown such a decided leaning towards the Jersey boy in their pre-fight stories.

But no one, not even Joe Gould and Doc Robb, realized that Braddock was so fine. No wonder then that newspaper opinion generally agreed that Loughran, who had been having trouble making the weight for over a year and who even away back in 1929 was considered near the end of his rope as a fighter, would be dethroned.

After all, had not this jarring young Braddock from Jersey the kick of a mule in his right hand? Had he not shattered Pete Latzo's jaw to fragments and then knocked out Tuffy Griffiths in two rounds and Jimmy Slattery in nine?

Admitting that he had blown a decision to Leo Lomski, had not this same Lomski fellow thrown a terrific scare into Loughran one night? Had not Lomski cracked Loughran with an overhand right that had sent the Philadelphian somersaulting to the canvas? Had not Loughran, after "somersaulting and then bouncing up on one knee," as Ed Sullivan of the New York Graphic described it, been knocked down again only a few seconds later? True enough, Philadelphia's Tommy had then gotten up and staged a marvelous exhibition to earn a decision in the later rounds. But would he be able to get up if Braddock ever hit him on the jaw as Lomski had? The answer, in view of the Griffiths and Slattery knockouts, was a decided "no."

And what about the weight problem? Wouldn't Loughran who already had a ring record of eleven years behind him in 1929, pay the penalty for torturing his body so mercilessly to make 175 pounds? Had he not been struggling for over a year with this same condition? Had he not announced that win or lose, he was going to give up his light-heavyweight title after the Braddock fight? Of course he had.

No wonder then that most of the critics thought Braddock would be crowned a new champion. In the face of an overwhelming vote for Braddock in the pre-fight pronouncements, very few critics felt Loughran had a chance. One of them, Joe Williams, of the New York *World-Telegram*, sounded the note for these few when he declared that "a gent who doesn't care to be hit isn't the easiest target known to man, woman or beast."

Mr. Williams, as it later turned out, had said a mouthful.

CHAPTER EIGHT

LOUGHRAN AND DEFEAT

TOMMY
LOUGHRAN

ONLY those who witnessed the fight can possibly appreciate the masterful performance that Tommy Loughran gave in crushing James J. Braddock that night in July, 1929. The defending champion literally left-handed Braddock to death and won twelve of the fifteen rounds. Braddock won all of two, and one round was considered even.

In the two rounds which were awarded Braddock, the champion suffered bad cuts. The fight was only a few seconds old when Braddock, with a short but terrific inside punch, opened a ghastly looking cut over Loughran's right eye.

Tumult filled the night air above the Stadium. Why, the fight had hardly started and here Loughran's eye was spouting blood like water out of a hydrant! A technical knockout seemed imminent, so profusely did the blood gush from the cut. In a desperate series of efforts to reach the eye again, Braddock now went "right hand crazy." Around the ring he tore after the bleeding Loughran. Blows thudded upon the champion from all angles. But through it all, the courageous fighter from Philadelphia managed to keep his head and finally he heard the welcome bell.

Any notion that Braddock might have had that Loughran was going the way of Slattery and Griffiths, however, was soon dispelled. The wound over his eye dressed, Loughran, himself once more, came out for the second round and then proceeded to administer a boxing exhibition that made Braddock look like the rawest kind of a novice.

Braddock swung one right after another. Loughran just danced around him and jabbed him, and then tied him into all kinds of knots when in close. And he talked to Braddock, too. First he praised Braddock. Then he taunted him. Then he let him have a stiff left between the eyes. The more he talked, the madder Braddock got, and the madder Braddock got, the more he missed and the more he missed the more he lurched ludicrously around the ring. By the sixth round, Braddock was even further behind than the turtle in that famous race with the hare.

In the opening moments of the seventh round, however, Braddock managed to get over one furious punch. It was a terrific right-hand wallop that Loughran was not able to back away from entirely because of the ropes. The blow, sweeping upward, grazed Loughran's nose and forehead and suddenly a mass of blood poured forth from a cut in almost the very middle of Tommy's forehead.

To this day, Loughran carries a visible memento of that punch.

Yet that blow did not distract Loughran as much as had the one in the first round. The champion signaled to his corner for his seconds to get ready to dress the cut. And then, stepping out, himself managed to land just before the heat ended a right that buckled Braddock's knees, believe it or not. Yes, the man from Philadelphia, who wasn't supposed to have a punch, landed in this round perhaps the hardest wallop of the fight.

Just once in those remaining rounds, before the fight rolled to its conclusion, did Braddock manage to land a stiff punch. This one was a thundering right, and it caught Loughran in the twelfth round, at a time when the champion's physical resources were at a dangerously low ebb.

"I had had a terrific ordeal making the weight," Loughran explained later. "After weighing in, I drank almost a gallon of beef bouillon and when I entered the ring, I must have weighed, around 185 pounds. For ten rounds, I felt swell. But then I started to go, and I was pretty well spent when Braddock clipped me with that smash in the twelfth.

"But I never let him realize my true condition. I kept talking to him. Had he known how I actually felt, it might have been too bad for me. But he didn't. I had to use my head there. He turned on one occasion to answer a taunt flung by a ringsider. I cuffed him with my left, and then getting in close and clinching, warned him never, never to do that again."

The going grew fearfully dull in the closing rounds. Jimmy just couldn't find Loughran. On one occasion, he hissed for Loughran "to come on and fight." Loughran retorted with two left jabs. Laboriously, poor Braddock plodded in, desperately trying to park his right hand where it would do some damage. No use. Loughran just blinded him with left jabs which were alternated with whirling, vicious uppercuts, punches with which Loughran was able to score effectively as Jimmy came in, head down.

When it was all over, Jimmy complained, as he had done once or twice before after losing a fight, that he did not know what had been wrong with him.

The answer was simple. One of the best, if not the best left hand in the profession, had handed him a decisive drubbing. In the years to come, Braddock finally realized what had happened—and when he did, the realization changed some of his boxing theories completely.

He paid the penalty, as he read the papers the next day, for having fallen down so miserably. All the newspaper accounts dilated on Braddock's deplorable slowness, while Loughran, on the other hand, was acclaimed rightly, as one of the greatest fighters ever to have appeared in a ring. Damon Runyon, of the *New York American*, wrote "the way Loughran boxed last night, he would probably have licked anybody around right now," and Ed Van Every, of the New York *Sun* (then of the lamented New York *Evening World*) declared that Loughran "displayed some stuff in the art of fisticuffs that was superior to the best work of Gene Tunney."

No wonder Braddock had looked like a novice. But in the years to come, many a critic conceded that the youngster from Jersey who had had only three years of professional experience when he faced Loughran, should not have been condemned so severely for his miserable showing against the Philadelphian.

Loughran himself sounded a significant note. Interviewed by Burris Jenkins, then cartoonist for the old New York *Evening World* and now on the staff of the New York *Evening Journal*, Tommy said in reply to queries regarding the bruises on his forehead and under and above his left eye:

"No, those weren't done with right hands. He didn't land his right solidly once on anything except my shoulder. These (pointing to the bruises) were the result of left hands. The kid has a good left hand. If he could only learn to box."

Strange are the workings of Fate. Years later, Braddock's left hand, of which Loughran had spoken so highly, defeated in succession, John Henry Lewis, Art Lasky, and then Max Adelbert Baer to win a world's heavyweight championship. And Loughran watched the last fight from a ringside seat.

CHAPTER NINE

MARRIAGE

MAE THERESA BRADDOCK

SOME six months after the Loughran fight, Braddock was married.

The young miss who had captured his heart was Mae Theresa Fox, telephone operator in a New York exchange, who lived in Guttenberg, New Jersey, only a few blocks away from the Braddock domicile, and whose brother, Howard, was, next to Marty McGann, perhaps, closer to Jim Braddock than anybody else. Not infrequently Howard Fox came home with Jimmy "for something to eat" and usually it was Mae Fox who set the table.

For years, Jim was a bashful, silent suitor. He had loved Mae Fox from the day he had met her. But he had never been able to muster enough courage to propose marriage.

It was not until after the Loughran fight in the summer of 1929, that he finally popped the question and to his perspiring relief, her answer was "yes." At that time, Braddock had amassed a young fortune of $30,000. He had about $10,000 in the bank and some $20,000 invested in stocks and bonds and a taxicab company which operated in West New York.

"I can afford to set up a nice home now," said Jimmy.

There was, however, some talk in the air of Braddock figuring in an outdoor fight and it was decided to wait until the winter to get married.

Braddock made a trip to the Pacific Coast in August. It resulted in nothing but a defeat at the hands of Yale Okun. He returned East and was signed to fight Maxie Rosenbloom at the Garden on November 15th, 1929. His fiancée came to witness this fight. There is an old saying about the course of true love never running smooth. So it was this night. James J. looked so positively awful against the Harlem Harlequin that Mae Fox, heartbroken, fled from the building long before the final round came around.

Braddock took a thorough hiding in the newspapers the next day. This time, he had looked so appallingly awkward and so unbearably slow, that the critics began writing his fistic obituary. The reaction to these items was not pleasant, it is safe to say.

"I'm disgusted with it all," said Jimmy to Mae. "Let's get married and I'll settle down. I'll devote all my time to the taxicab business."

They decided to get married immediately after the Christmas holidays. Saturday, January 18th, 1930, was set as the date for the wedding.

Showing little concern for the marital desires of his fighter, however, little Joe Gould forced a postponement of the wedding—on account of a fight, strange though such a statement may sound.

About ten days before the scheduled wedding, Gould got Braddock on the 'phone.

"Get busy," he said, "you're going to fight Leo Lomski again—this time in Chicago."

"When?" asked Braddock.

"January 17th," replied Gould.

Braddock was silent. "Gee whiz, Joe," he finally said, "that's the night before my wedding."

"Well, I can't postpone the fight on account of a wedding, but you might postpone your wedding on account of a fight," countered Gould. "We're getting $6,000 from Jack Dempsey (who was then promoting at the Coliseum in Chicago) for this one. You can use that kind of money, can't you? And if we lick Lomski this time . . . ."

"I'll take a plane right back after the fight on Friday night and I'll be back here in plenty of time for the wedding Saturday," Braddock pleaded with Mae.

"Nothing doing," replied Mae very pertly and very firmly.

"Suppose you get a black eye. Do you think I want to walk up the aisle with a bridegroom who has a black eye? I do not. No, Jim, we'll postpone the wedding for a week."

So one week later than originally scheduled—on January 25th, 1930, at 9 :30 in the morning, at a Mass at St. Joseph's of the Palisades Roman Catholic Church, in West New York, James J. Braddock and Mae Theresa Fox were married. The bridegroom was a positive picture of health and carried no black eyes. And Mae Theresa was a distinctly lovely bride.

There was a little sequel to the Lomski fight which necessitated a postponement of Jimmy Braddock's wedding. It came in the form of a letter which arrived at Joe Gould's office on January 27th, 1930, just ten days after the fight, and just two days after the wedding.

The communication was from the Illinois Athletic Commission. It informed Gould that the draw decision rendered at the conclusion of the Lomski fight had been rescinded and that Lomski had been declared the winner!

Gould's reply to the commission was a gem. It read:

"I have received from you today a letter notifying me that Lomski has been declared the winner over Braddock ten days after the fight. May I and Braddock, who has just been married, thank you for the wedding present? We expect to hear any day now that Gene Tunney has at last been counted out in his fight with Jack Dempsey."

CHAPTER TEN

THE DECLINE OF A FIGHTER

THE years 1930, 1931 and 1932, though full of wedded bliss and marital happiness, were, in other respects, agonizing ones for James J. Braddock.

The depression, which had gripped the country, hit Braddock a staggering blow. Not only did all of his investments vanish into thin air, but whatever cash he had on hand was poured endlessly into his taxicab business in an effort to keep it going. Meanwhile, personal expenses--what with the arrival of new faces in the family, mounted rapidly.

To add to his steadily mounting problems, Braddock's fistic fortunes began to hit bedrock, too.

The descent, after the Rosenbloom and Lomski fights, was rapid. Before 1930 passed into history, he had lost to Billy Jones, in Philadelphia, to Babe Hunt, in Boston and to Harold Mays, at West New York. He did manage, however, to knock out Phil Mercurio in two rounds and decisioned Joe Monte in ten rounds. Both fights occurred in Boston.

Early in 1931, he met Ernie Schaaf at the Garden. Schaaf outweighed him, 207 to 178. In spite of the terrific handicap, Braddock waged the fiercest kind of a battle. But he lost the decision though the newspapers did wrangle over the verdict for several days. Joe Sekyra then whipped him in a tenner in New York. Al Gainer did likewise in a bout in New Haven. Andy Mitchell held him to a draw at Detroit. Shortly after that fight, he made the sad mistake of going against Maxie Rosenbloom again, this time in Minneapolis, and the thing looked so bad that it was stopped in the second round and declared no contest. His lone victories in 1931 were registered over Jack Roper, whom he knocked out in one round in Miami, in March, and Jack Kelly, whom he outpointed in ten rounds at Waterbury, Conn., during the same month.   March was living nobly up to its reputation of being a lucky month for him.

In 1932, he won only two fights, no more and no less than he had been able to register in 1931 and 1930. Oddly enough, as in those years, so in 1932 he won one fight by a knockout and one fight by a decision. His kayo victory was scored in New York over Vincent Parille, a hard-hitting Argentine with a terrific wallop. The tussle lasted five rounds. His decision triumph over the ten round route was over Dynamite Jackson at San Diego, California. Jackson, a few years later, was to serve as a sparring partner for Max Baer.

His defeats in 1932 were many and they were many because the financial plight in which he was beginning to find himself now began to affect his boxing in a marked degree. The remnants of his fortune of almost $30,000 were swept away during 1932. The taxicab business had long since folded up. Failure to carry an adequate amount of insurance had resulted in several attachments, too.

Five fighters defeated him on points and a sixth scored a technical knockout over him that year. Baxter Calmes, Charley Retzlati and Tony Shucco defeated him in bouts in the East, while John Henry Lewis and

Tom Patrick whaled out decisions over him on the Coast later. In the Patrick fight, he suffered a bad cut over the eye. Half a dozen stitches were required when it was sewed together after the fight.

Just eighteen days later, on November 9th, he grabbed at the opportunity to jump in as a substitute against Lou Scozza of Buffalo, at San Francisco, because the purse meant railroad fare back home. Early in that fight, Scozza opened the cut suffered in the Patrick fight and eventually, in the sixth round, the referee halted the proceedings despite Braddock's entreaties, giving Scozza a technical knockout over Braddock—the only knockout of any kind charged against the Jerseyite.

After going along three successive years with only two victories to show for each year, Braddock scored four victories in 1933. Before the year was out, however, he was not only going to meet several reverses as well, but also was to break his hand and be thrown out of the ring on one occasion—an occasion which he believed, at the time, was his farewell appearance as a fighter.

His first victory of 1933 was registered on January 13th. In that bout he stopped the sensational rise of young Martin Levandowski, a brilliant young fighter who had come out of the amateur ranks and then proceeded to run riot through the professionals.

Braddock must have instinctively thought of Tuffy Griffiths when he left for Chicago, where the fight was to take place. For Levandowski, he was informed, had a record of 36 knockouts to his credit, one over none other than Bob Olin. His opponent's knockout record did not disturb him but a pronouncement by the Illinois Athletic Commission upon his arrival in the Windy City, did. The solons politely informed Braddock that he would not be permitted to go on with Levandowski unless he first displayed his wares in a gymnasium. The boxing fathers were not going to be parties to any massacres—not if they could help it.

Braddock, of course, had no alternative. He readily agreed to do his stuff in a gym, and one afternoon, as the solons looked critically on, he lit into Larry Johnson and Seal Harris so furiously that the commissioners quickly agreed a match between Levandowski and Braddock would not be so one-sided after all.

As it turned out, however, the bout did prove one-sided. Only instead of being in Levandowski's, it was in Braddock's favor. As the gong sounded, the comparatively short and chunky Levandowski sailed into Braddock with both arms flying, quite confident that James J. would be his 37th victim. But before he knew it, he had been punched to the deck no less than five times and taken a most thorough pasting from Braddock.

Our hero returned East feeling quite pleased with himself.

"Them knockout sensations," he said elegantly to Joe Gould, "are my meat."

A few weeks later he figured in an automobile accident while riding with a friend and suffered several broken ribs. The injuries had not healed as yet when Gould signed him to fight Hans Birkie, in New York. Rather than blow the purse, Braddock went through with the fight. Birkie won. In the bargain, Braddock hurt his hand.

Shortly afterwards, on March 1st, 1933, he journeyed to Philadelphia, to meet Al Ettore. His hand was still bad and Ettore, a hard man to fight, made Jimmy look dreadful. So much so that the referee heaved Braddock out of the ring in the fourth round, and reported to the

Pennsylvania solons that our hero had displayed a shameful lack of ambition. The solons refused to pay any attention to the claim that Braddock had a bad hand, and a suspension, which included Joe Gould, too, followed.

Ten years before, a Gene Tunney-Jack Renault bout in the Sleepy City had been stopped in the fourth round, too. And Tunney not only had lived it down, but four years later had won the world's heavyweight championship. Strange as it may sound, the Braddock who was chased from a Philadelphia ring in 1933 was to duplicate Gene Tunney's feat and win the same championship himself a few years later.

Three weeks after the Ettore thing he bobbed up in St. Louis to fight Al Stillman. Stillman was another one of "those knockout sensations."

He had just scored an overwhelming victory over Max Rosenbloom—of all fighters—and had punctured that noteworthy feat with no less than three knockdowns. As a result, he ruled a three-to-one favorite when Braddock arrived in the Mound City. And by fight time, the odds went as high as six to one.

Braddock, however, managed to get by. For nine rounds, the two men staged a whirlwind battle. But in the tenth and final round, Braddock laid a terrific right-hand smash to the youngster's jaw and Stillman was finished; The blow, however, all but broke Jim's hand again.

The tide began to swirl against Braddock after that fight. On April 5th he met Levandowski in a return bout, this time at St. Louis, and lost in 10 rounds. And on May 19th, he met Stillman again—also in St. Louis. Again he lost. His hand was "shot" and he looked completely dejected.

Those two defeats killed him as a card in the Midwest. But he was in dire need of money. He began to look for action in his home county. He fought Les Kennedy, the Californian, at the old Oakland Arena, in Jersey City, on June 21st, and scored a victory on points. Four weeks later, on July 21st, he fought and licked Chester Matan in similar fashion at the West New York Playgrounds. His right hand was "coked" for both fights.

Then came the Abe Feldman fight in Mount Vernon, N. Y., which was ruled no contest, which saw him this time actually break the hand and which apparently wrote *finis* to his boxing career. The Feldman scrap took place on September 25th, 1933. The first round was spent in feeling one another out, but in the second, Feldman came to Jimmy—and Jimmy, seeing an opening, planted his right on Feldman's noggin. Feldman's noggin refused to give, but Jimmy's dope-laden right did and he winced as he felt a bolt of pain. He knew instantly that the jig was up—that he had broken the hand again.

Dismayed and desperate, he tried to carry on with his left. But fighters with two good hands had found Feldman tough to handle, and Braddock, trying to fight him with one, looked pitiful. The gallery gods, little realizing what had happened, soon began to clap their hands and whistle and jeer. Finally, in the middle of the sixth round, the referee, announcing that "enough was enough," threw both men out of the ring and declared the bout "no contest." The purses were ordered held up and the fighters were instructed to appear before the commission.

At the meeting of the New York Commission, however, doctors' examinations revealed what had happened to Braddock—and the fistic fathers, almost apologetically, turned over the purse which had been held up. But though the purse came in handy, and the absolution by the fistic fathers erased whatever stigma the Mount Vernon bounce may have cast upon Jimmy's record, our hero left the commission's offices with a heavy heart. The doctors had informed him that it would be many, many months before the hand would heal.

"I guess I'm all washed up now," he sighed to Gould. Joe was too glum to make any answer. They walked out of the State Building in silence and Braddock headed back to Jersey a completely discouraged person indeed.

CHAPTER ELEVEN

RELIEF CASE No. 2796

JIMMY BRADDOCK never will forget Christmas, 1933.

His luck had wallowed right to rock bottom by the holidays. Now and then, friends who saw him sitting about at the North Bergen club, now looking drearily into space and now at his right hand imbedded in a cast, pitied him and asked him to "have a beer." Jimmy never refused. There were many days when he had nothing but those beers for sustenance.

Five or six weeks elapsed before the cast on his hand was taken off. In a desperate effort to keep a roof over his head, he then sought work on the docks at Weehawken—but work was scarce. Some weeks he labored two days, and some weeks three days. Some weeks he made ten or twelve dollars but there were many other weeks during which the income failed to total any more than five dollars. To top it all off, the winter of 1933-34 proved to be one of the most severe in decades. Things came to a complete standstill as snow and ice choked the streets and railroads.

Desperately Braddock tried to struggle through those terrible, cold months. But steadily, his plight grew worse. A wife and three children were looking to him for support and Jimmy just couldn't get work. Rose Marie, only a few months old, needed careful attention and plenty of milk. For that matter, so, too, did Jay, his first child, who was born in January, 1931, and Howard, his second youngster, who had come about a year later. The children had to be clothed, too. Rent had to be paid.

Daily, Braddock trudged the snow-laden streets looking for something else to do when the "No Work Today" sign confronted him at the railroad yards. His clothes were worn to the seams now. He usually was noticed shuffling around in a faded old green sweater and a pair of trousers that had long since seen their best days. There were holes in his shoes. He discouragedly roamed the streets with his hands in his pockets. And his pockets were empty.

Only a few, very close intimates knew how badly off Jimmy really was. He generally forced a smile in the presence of friends. Now and then he picked up some change tending bar in the North Bergen Social and Athletic Club. But very few of those who saw him there realized just how viciously misfortune was searing his soul.

If things had been dark and dreary during the winter, they not only failed to improve with the advent of spring but, because of the bills which he had piled up, actually became worse. He was behind in his rent, the milk bill had run past $25, and his gas and electric bills also had reached big proportions.

Creditors soon began to make life completely unbearable. He was forced to vacate the apartment, in which he had been living, and move into a smaller one in the same building. But now the milkman was insistent on payment. He had stretched things as far as he could. To top it all off, the news came one day that unless the gas and electric bill was paid—there wouldn't be any more gas and electric for the Braddocks.

By this time, Jimmy had borrowed from almost every available source. He had long since reached that stage where he had noted with pangs in his heart that his fair-weather friends invariably crossed to the other side of the street when they saw him coming. In desperation, he decided to go to New York and see if Joe Gould could lend him $35 with which to pay the milkman and something on the electric bill.

He still recalls that trip across the Hudson River.

He had just one, thin dime in his pocket as he headed for New York. He walked from Woodcliff to the West Shore Ferry. The fare across was four cents. Jimmy was still six cents to the good. Once on the other side, he walked up 42nd Street, turned left on Eighth Avenue, and trudged to the Garden.

In those days, Gould, having a tussle with the old wolf himself, used to make his "office" in the Garden. Mail intended for him was addressed to him there. Telephone calls for him were received there, too. And at least once a day, Gould appeared at the Garden to see "if anything was doing," and, of course, to listen to the Oracle of Eighth Avenue, Jimmy Johnston.

Braddock had a long wait for Gould that afternoon, and Francis Albertanti, then press agent for the Garden, finally gave up after a heroic effort to conduct a conversation with Silent Jim.

"Have a seat until Gould comes," Albertanti said.

Braddock sat down. And Albertanti, shaking his head over his failure to get any more than "uh-huh" out of Braddock, went back to work.

Late in the afternoon, Gould appeared on the scene.

"What's up, Jim?" he asked.

They went out into the hallway.

"I've got to have $35, Joe," said Braddock. "Can you get it for me?"

Despite his snappy appearance (Gould always managed to keep up a good "front" no matter what the circumstances), Joe no more had $35 in his pocket than he had the Hope Diamond. He had taken to selling car radios to make ends meet—but precious few persons were buying either cars or radios in those days. He whistled as Jim asked for $35.

"Gee whiz, Jim," he said, "that's a lot of money. But wait a minute."

Shortly afterwards, he reappeared with the $35.

"Here," he directed, "go ahead and pay the milk bill. I made a touch upstairs. And keep in shape. Things can't go on like this forever. I'll get something for you yet."

Braddock walked back to the ferry, shelled out four pennies for a return fare, and then hoofed slowly up the hill where he stopped off and made a payment on the electric bill, after which he headed for North Bergen and paid the milkman.

The Braddock kids got their milk the next day.

But the $35 which Joe Gould had dug up for the milkman and the electric bill saved Jim only temporarily. Four or five weeks later, he again was in arrears. Creditors began pressing him once more. He might have tried Gould again—but he knew that Joe needed money almost as badly as he did.

For a long time, Braddock, unable to get any kind of work anywhere, refused to go to the authorities for aid. But finally, when conditions became absolutely unbearable, there was nothing else to do.

The world at large will little know what Braddock suffered before he applied for relief. Only those who have been in the same desperate predicament—and not a few who had been later made it a point to write the most encouraging letters to him at Loch Sheldrake where he trained for the Baer fight—can possibly appreciate what he went through. It was only when the notice came again that the gas and electric supply would be cut off and the milkman regretfully declared he couldn't extend any more credit that Braddock, despair and discouragement engraved upon his face, applied to the municipal authorities for aid.

By a strange coincidence, the relief problems of the township of North Bergen were under the supervision of Township Commissioner Harry Buesser, who some ten years before had acted as Braddock's second the night Jimmy had fought his first fight in a ring, under the name of "Jimmy Ryan." And Joe Kelly, of Buesser's department, who also took an interest in the fighter's case, was the same Joe Kelly who only a few years back had covered some of Jimmy's fights for the *Hudson Dispatch*. His brother, Jimmy Kelly, relief investigator, handled Braddock's case.

The usual relief allotment for a man and wife was $7.65 every two weeks. Wherever there were children in the family, however, extra grants were made. Braddock, with three children to feed, was given slightly over double the usual grant. He stayed on relief for something like nine months in all. In that time, he drew a little over $300 from the authorities.

Braddock never forgot that debt to society. A year or so later, in March of 1935, when, thanks to an amazing series of occurrences and a startling left hand which had been nurtured on privation and hard labor, he succeeded in collecting a purse of $4,100 for beating Art Lasky, the first thing he did was to send a check to the authorities discharging the debt—and closing his "case."

CHAPTER TWELVE

METAMORPHOSIS

IT was during the period he was on relief that the metamorphosis of James J. Braddock took place.

Up until the night he broke his right hand on Abe Feldman, in September, 1933, James J. Braddock always had favored the use of that hand, a natural thing to do in view of some of the startling knockouts he had scored with it. At certain times in his career, when forced to do so, he had fallen back upon his left hand and plied his way to victory. But those were rare instances.

As it was, it finally required a broken hand, and a compelling force of circumstances that followed, to develop Braddock's left to a point where it became weapon enough to carry him to a world's heavyweight championship.

Not until after he had scored his sensational victory over Art Lasky, did newspapermen, conducting what almost amounted to an inquisition in an effort to find out how Braddock (strictly a right-hand puncher as far back as they remembered) had developed the potency of his left, discover the secret. "Swinging the tie-hook did it," Jimmy explained to Walter St. Denis, veteran New York sports editor, one day.

When Braddock broke his right hand on Feldman's head and decided he was through with the ring, he turned to long-shoring, not an unusual occupation for a big fellow. Off and on during the year that followed, he labored at the railroad yards in Weehawken, loading and unloading ties, whenever the opportunity offered.

The work was hard. The men usually stripped to the waist. The ties were lifted by means of a tie-hook, something after the fashion of a bale-hook. A swift, punching motion sinks the end of this hook into the tie and enables the long-shoreman to lift and carry his end.

Braddock, holding the hook with his right hand, (which had just come out of a cast) found the first time that he threw it into a tie that he was going to have trouble. A stinging pain shot through the "hand. The mitt had rebelled.

There was only one thing to do. He had to turn to his left hand. He did.

It was the turning point in his career—but neither Jimmy nor anybody else knew it at the time.

The months rolled by. When Jimmy could not get work on the wharves, he applied elsewhere. He labored in a coal yard for a spell. He worked on a moving van. He tended bar. He did half a dozen other things—but most of the time he was down at the docks in Weehawken, swinging a hook with his left hand, loading ties onto lighters.

And that swinging of the tie-hook, giving his left arm a vigorous, punching exercise, worked wonders within a few months. The arm grew stronger and stronger. He began to rely more and more upon his left.

And when Old Man Opportunity came knocking on his door a few months later, he opened the door, as it were, with that left hand.

Braddock's improvement was not confined strictly to the development of his left, either.

By June, 1934, the Jerseyite, though out of the ring for something like nine months and subsisting through the greater part of that stretch on nothing but a daily diet of hash, was in remarkable physical trim—as hard as nails, so to speak.

For the hard labor around the docks and the continual walking about not only while at work—but even more so hunting work, had made a new man out of Jimmy.

His home was in North Bergen and daily he walked back and forth to the West Shore railroad yards, over three miles away. Sometimes he made this trip twice a day. Whenever he failed to catch on at the West Shore, he would tramp up the river to West New York, or Edgewater, and not infrequently, he would journey over to Brooklyn after work. He was ring rusty, yes, but his body was lean and trim. His eyes were clear. His legs were sturdy.

On an afternoon in June, 1934, while he was sweating away on one of the wharves, Braddock felt somebody tap him on the shoulder.

He turned around and was surprised to see Joe Gould smiling at him.

"Well, champ," was Gould's breezy greeting, "I've got a fight for you."

Braddock smiled. He had not heard such pleasant news in a long, long time.

"But the fight takes place Thursday night of this week," Gould continued. "You've got only two days. Are you in shape?"

"Am I in shape?" retorted Braddock. "Look at me."

Gould was forced to admit his fighter seemed to be in splendid condition.

"Well, you had better hustle over to Stillman's tomorrow anyway, and get at least one workout in," concluded Gould.

"I'll meet you there."

"Er-er, wait a minute," said Braddock. "Any chance of getting a little cash in advance?"

"I'll see what I can do," said Gould. "I'm going over to the Garden now."

Later in the day, Jimmy Johnston, the Madison Square Garden matchmaker, okayed an advance of $100 out of the purse of $250 which Braddock was to get for fighting Corn Griffin on the Primo Carnera-Max Baer world's heavyweight championship card. Gould and Braddock split the $100 down the middle on Wednesday and on Thursday night, Braddock, a couple of substantial meals behind him, stepped into the ring against Corn Griffin for the first of three fights that were destined to make him a challenger for the world's heavyweight championship.

Corn Griffin was a private in the United States Army when Charles Harvey, walrus-mustached fight manager, discovered him. So enthused was Harvey over the soldier's prospects that he effected Griffin's resignation from the service and began directing him up the fistic ladder.

After several successful fights here and there, Harvey brought Corn to New York. Shortly afterwards, he hired the southerner out as a spar mate for Primo Carnera, who was training at Pompton Lakes for the Baer fight. Griffin looked pretty nifty at Pompton—and won a place on the Carnera-Baer card.

All that was needed now was an opponent—an opponent with "a name" as Jimmy Johnston and Harvey both put it—somebody with a bit of a reputation, somebody with whom Griffin would not have too much trouble and at whose expense (it was fondly hoped) Griffin would be able to somersault into the limelight.

Johnston and Harvey had their heads together in Johnston's inner office at the Garden one day when Joe Gould's voice. was heard outside. Gould had dropped in to ask Margie Regan, Johnston's secretary, if there had been "any telephone calls today?"

"I've got it," exclaimed Johnston, "the man we want for Griffin is Braddock."

"Right," agreed Harvey gleefully. "He'll be easy for Griffin. He hasn't fought in a year."

Gould, however, as desperately as he needed the money, showed some reluctance about pitting Braddock against Griffin who was said to have a rattling good punch.

"How about giving us Dynamite Jackson?" he countered. "He's knocking hell out of Baer down at Asbury Park, isn't he? We'll fight him. That ought to be a good match."

Jackson had been showing astonishing form against the challenger for Carnera's title in the workouts at Asbury. But the real reason Gould wanted to fight Jackson was because Braddock had beaten Jackson in 1932, in a bout on the Coast, and Gould figured Jimmy could repeat in 1935.

But Johnston was incensed at the suggestion.

"You're always on my neck for a bout for that washed-up heavyweight of yours," he exploded, "but when I give you one—you turn around and offer to fight somebody else. Well, you'll fight Griffin or you won't fight at all."

Mr. Braddock fought Griffin.

That fight proved the turning point of Jimmy Braddock's career— the final appearance of light after months and months of darkness, gloom and misery.

Over 56,000 persons had crowded into the Garden's Long Island City Bowl on the night of June 14th, 1934 to see Baer lift the championship from Carnera in that abysmal battle in which Carnera hit the deck eleven times all told and which finally ended in a technical knockout in the 11th round with Baer as the new champion.

There was drama in that championship fight that night. But as far as New Jersey was concerned, the drama occurred in one of the preliminaries in which James J. Braddock, who had been forced to roll his trunks up in an old newspaper and who had borrowed a pair of fighting shoes for the night, knocked Corn Griffin out in three rounds and started a march that was within one year to put him in the same ring as a challenger for the title which Baer was about to win.

As in the Battle of Life, in which he was floored during 1933 and 1934, only to get up, so he did this night against Corn Griffin.

Griffin won the first round by the proverbial mile. Braddock was ring rusty. He was outboxed widely. And he realized early that he must get to Corn quickly—or else.

He was becoming firmly convinced that this alone was his salvation— when Griffin suddenly cracked him on the jaw with a pulverizing right hand punch and sent him tumbling to the canvas. It seemed as though he would never get up. He rolled around, badly hurt, and over in Griffin's corner, the walrus-mustached Harvey began to envision the screaming headline—"Corn Griffin knocks out James J. Braddock."

But Harvey never saw that headline. He saw, instead, one which proclaimed the knockout of Griffin by James J. Braddock.

Yes, this family man from North Bergen, who now was 28 years old, who had a wife and three children, who had not fought in nine months, who had broken his hand in his last fight, and who had subsisted for months on nothing but hash, got up after taking a count of nine, marched grimly into Griffin and hit the southerner with a short, inside right to the jaw that sent Corn down for nine. Griffin never got over that punch. He fought the rest of the round in a daze.

Desperately, Griffin tried to evade Braddock's finishing wallop as the third began. But Braddock was marching to a championship now, even though he did not know it. Something pushed him on. Eventually he landed two more thundering right hand smashes and Griffin was through for the night, Referee McPartland stopping the fight after two minutes and 37 seconds of the third round.

Gould just bubbled over with exultation as he led Braddock to the dressing room.

"That was great," he murmured over and over again. "That was great. You certainly stiffened him in style."

"Aw, that was nothing," grinned Jimmy. "I did that on hash. Wait until I get a couple of hamburgers in me and I'll show them something!"

Very soon, however, Jimmy had to go back to the docks in search of work. The $150 which he and Gould had split after the fight was eaten up quickly, debts taking the greater portion. June ran into July and July into August. Soon autumn came and the frost began to chill the pumpkin.

Braddock was up against it again. He recalled only too vividly the previous winter and little did he care to go through another one like it. He had not heard from Gould in weeks. Yes, he had knocked Corn Griffin into oblivion. But no one in New York was recalling that victory. It had been forgotten almost as it had been scored. The talk of New York since the night of June 14th, 1934 was Max Baer who was being labelled quite positively as the "greatest fighter since Dempsey."

At this particular time, Jackie Farrell, who years before had served as sports editor of the *Hudson Dispatch* and who later for a period of almost ten years had been boxing editor of the New York *Daily News*, was running a fight club at Columbia Amusement Park, located in Braddock's own township of North Bergen.

Good matches were scarce and Farrell was having a rocky time. One fine day he hit upon the idea of matching Braddock with Steve Dudas, a young Jersey heavyweight who had built up quite a reputation in New York rings. Braddock fell over himself agreeing when Farrell broached him with the suggestion. Here was a chance to get enough money to go through the winter.

"We'll stage the fight under the auspices of the North Bergen Social and Athletic Club," Farrell declared. "And we'll all make a buck."

But Farrell and Braddock found Dudas' managers, Freddie and John Huber (in whose cellar years before, Braddock had first picked up the rudiments of boxing) lukewarm.

"Ah, the match von't draw," John Huber protested in his pronounced accent. "Steef and Chimmy are both members of the North Bergen club. The public von't come out to see them fight. They're such goot friends."

The truth really was that John Huber hesitated about sending his young fighter against Braddock. While a victory over a "name" fighter such as Braddock was not to be sneezed at—there were hazards. Others might have forgotten, but John Huber remembered almost every knockout that the lad who had first started to box in his cellar, had scored. And he had seen Braddock get up off the canvas only a few months before to knock out Corn Griffin.

It took almost three weeks of pleading by Farrell and Braddock and some considerable pressure by members of the North Bergen club, too, before the boys finally met one afternoon in the clubrooms and signed to fight. Joe Gould was not present: Braddock was engineering this match himself.

"Look," Braddock pleaded with John Huber before John finally signed, "my right hand is shot. I've had only one fight in over a year and I guess it's all over with me as far as boxing is concerned. But I just want this fight to get me enough dough to go through the winter."

Huber was still doubtful as to the wisdom of the match, but he had an inkling of Braddock's personal distress and finally gave in—even though he did shake his head as he signed, fearing the match would not draw because Steve and Jimmy were "such goot friends."

The fight was set for late in November and Braddock and Dudas began training. Soon, the North Bergen club became divided into two camps. Before long, heavy wagers had been placed—and those who were betting on Braddock began to show keen interest in Jimmy's condition.

"Outside of those three rounds with Griffin, you haven't done a thing in over a year," they pounded away at Jimmy. "This Dudas has boxed almost every other week. He's in great fighting trim and unless you get into shape, you're going to be in for a licking."

The news that Dudas was working extra hard himself for the fight, finally roused Braddock to action. He began to hit the road every morning for six or seven miles, his friends trouping right along with him. And every afternoon in the North Bergen club's midget ring he boxed with fellows like Johnny Duff and Pat Sullivan, a North Bergen copper who was quite an amateur fighter.

Within a few weeks, Braddock had whipped himself into the best condition he had been in for years. The hard labor on the docks, and some real training, had worked wonders. He really was in splendid fettle for Steve Dudas.

But the Dudas fight never came off.

For just about ten days or so before the clash was to have taken place, Braddock got a telephone call at the North Bergen club. Joe Gould was on the wire—to tell him that he had just signed him to fight John Henry Lewis, of California, in a ten-round semi-final to the Max Rosenbloom—Bob Olin light-heavyweight championship scrap at Madison Square Garden!

"Johnston wants to know whether you're in shape for such a fight," explained Gould. "Have you been doing any training?"

"Plenty," replied Braddock. "I've been training two weeks now for a fight with Steve Dudas."

"Well, you'll have to postpone that," said Gould. "This is a big opportunity we've got with Lewis."

The Dudas match, of course, was cancelled—and Hudson County's sporting world bemoaned that cancellation, for it ruined the county's only indoor fight club.

Who dreamt at the time that the series of events which had culminated in the cancellation were but preliminary steps in the crowning of a world's heavyweight champion?

In the estimation of those who had seen the majority of his fights for a period of over ten years, James J. Braddock turned in the most brilliant performance of his entire career in whipping John Henry Lewis on the night of November 16th, 1934, at Madison Square Garden. Only the fact that in the bout which followed this performance, Bob Olin, of New York, overthrew Maxie Rosenbloom as the world's light-heavyweight champion, shunted newspaper attention away from Braddock's exhibition.

As had been the case when he was thrown in against Corn Griffin, Braddock was given the shot at John Henry Lewis in the fervent hope that he would prove an excellent "stooge" for the Negro, who only two years before, in September, 1932, had beaten him in a bout in San Francisco.

But Lewis soon found out that the Braddock of 1932 and the Braddock of 1934 were two different entities. The Braddock of 1932 had no left hand. The Braddock of 1934 seemed to be all left hand.

Nevertheless, Lewis, a very clever boxer, had the edge in the first four rounds. But in the opening moments of the fifth round, a terrific left hand exploded sharply against his jaw and sent the amazed and dazed Negro sprawling to the canvas for a count of five.

Lewis was never the same after that knockdown.

The Garden rocked continually with excitement as Braddock, giving a surprising exhibition of boxing, fought the Negro at his own game to nab the decision. Even so, a low punch by Lewis (it cost the Negro a round) had to figure in deciding the fight, and the newspapers the next day, though they did give Braddock due praise for his showing, by no means agreed that he had been entitled to the decision—his fifth-round knockdown and a low blow by Lewis notwithstanding. That is how close the fight was.

Braddock thanked his lucky stars as that fight neared its finish that he had trained so arduously for Steve Dudas. For in view of the closeness of the struggle, even the faintest let-up or the slightest sign of weariness in those later rounds, would have cost him the decision, and perhaps obliterated him from the fistic picture forever. But hard labor on the docks whenever the opportunity offered and two weeks of road work for Dudas at the insistence of his friends, had given him two great legs and on those legs, he calmly, almost magnificently, boxed to victory. His calmness in the tensest moments amazed everybody at the ringside and Sam Taub, veteran fight broadcaster, harped between more than one round on the startling change in the "once right-hand crazy" fighter from Jersey. He was to exhibit the same desired calm some eight months later in the most important fight of his life.

The Lewis fight dumped a purse of some $700 into the laps of Braddock and Gould—and Gould made the $700 go a long way—even if a judgment of $250 did take a jarring slice out of the purse before he got busy. The first thing Gould did was to tog Braddock out in some nifty suits. Others might not have been giving it a thought, but Gould now was beginning to envision Braddock as a possible contender for the heavyweight championship at last. And he wanted Jimmy to look the part. The suspicion exists that Jimmy had surprised even his manager.

Braddock now started to eat regularly, too. He began to put away steaks. His lean frame had been demanding some solid nutrition for some months. Now he began to feed it.

"Take care of yourself and keep in shape," Gould advised. "Our luck has changed at last. I can feel it in my bones."

Daily, Gould began to visit Jimmy Johnston's offices. Daily, Braddock did likewise. While Gould would march into Johnston's inner sanctum for the high palavering, Braddock would deposit himself on the bench opposite Francis Albertanti's desk outside.

Johnston would mutter under his breath every time he passed Braddock.

"You've spoiled two guys for me," he protested one day.

"Well?" replied Braddock.

CHAPTER THIRTEEN

MAKING THE LASKY MATCH

JIMMY
JOHNSTON

SOME highly poignant maneuvers that struck a new note for even the fight game, preceded the making of the Lasky-Braddock match. Before he clinched the Lasky shot for his fighter, Joe Gould was called upon to display his finest managerial acumen. A series of circumstances of the weirdest pattern were to do the rest.

As John J. Romano, a prominent critic and editor of the *Post Boxing Guide*, remarked later in comparing Gould with Jack Kearns to the former's great advantage, "it was one thing to have a fighter like Dempsey in tow and another to have one like Braddock.

With a fighter like Dempsey, all Kearns had to do was to sit tight, sift through the flood of offers, and pick out the best. Even then, Kearns, it is considered, muffed badly when he refused to accept a percentage for the Carpentier fight, allowed the Harry Wills fight to slip through his fingers and also took Dempsey to fight Gibbons out in Shelby where he ran into all sorts of difficulties and even a little gun play before he collected Dempsey's purse."

Gould, of course, had in Braddock no such man-eater as Kearns had had in Dempsey. It always had been necessary for Gould to steer carefully in order to land Jimmy in the best possible "spots." And never was careful steering more imperative than in December of 1934.

The Garden around this time had decided upon a series of "eliminations" to determine the challenger for Max Baer's championship. Primo Carnera, Max Schmeling, Art Lasky, Steme Hamas, and Big Ray Impellitiere were among those who were to compete in the eliminations. Gould decided early that the man for Braddock to fight out of that crowd was Art Lasky—for several reasons.

For one thing, he felt that Braddock would have a better chance of licking Lasky than any of the others. For another thing, he felt that Lasky, who had come out of Minnesota, and who had rolled up a terrific record on the Coast, was the favorite of the Garden as an opponent for Baer. This was not entirely correct—the Garden had leanings towards Schmeling, who was in Germany at the time—but Gould reasoned that anybody who licked Lasky, who was the leading contender at the time in many eyes, would automatically become the leading contender himself.

Peculiarly enough, the Lasky crowd desired Braddock for an opponent, too. Better to mingle with this veteran than the likes of Carnera, Hamas or Schmeling, the Lasky cabinet figured.

One might suppose that under the circumstances the match would have been closed without a toot. But there was a hitch—and the hitch was Jimmy Johnston, who was beginning to suspect that perhaps this Braddock fellow was not so lucky after all. The victory which Braddock had scored over John Henry Lewis had impressed Johnston tremendously, and he was not at all sure that he would not be taking a chance on exploding Lasky, who was a good deal slower than Lewis, by throwing him in with Braddock. So, he parried as Gould kept demanding Lasky, day after day.

"How about Al Gainer? How about somebody else before Lasky?" he would fire back.

But Gould stuck to his guns. He had made up his mind that it meant everything in the world to Braddock to get Lasky in the ring with him—and how true his judgment was he was to discover only a few months later. And eventually, Johnston, listening to the confident Lasky crowd, began to believe that perhaps he had been underestimating Lasky after all, and out came the contracts.

Johnston closed with Gould for Braddock to fight Art Lasky on February 1st, 1935.

But on the very afternoon of the fight, poor Lasky was stricken with pleurisy and the tussle was called off to the sharp disappointment of Gould and Braddock, both of whom by this time were again sparring with the wolf at the door. There was nothing to do, however, but swallow—and wait. Lasky really was a very sick man. Braddock visited him at his hotel, posed for pictures, wished Lasky a speedy recovery for more reasons than one and then took his leave.

Facing perhaps two more lean months as the result of the postponement, Braddock was dejected indeed as he headed back for Jersey. It was bad enough to run into a postponement—but to run into one on the very afternoon of the fight—that was worse. How was he to know, however, that Fate was playing a trump card for him when she prevented the Lasky fight from going on per schedule? That sudden illness was to take plenty out of Lasky.

When Lasky and his managers, without setting a new date for the fight, left a week later for the Coast, where Lasky was to recuperate, Gould was furious.

"What do they think they've got here, anyway?" he demanded of Johnston. "I've got to know what's what. I tell you they're giving me the run-around. They're afraid of Braddock."

Actually, Lasky's managers still felt Braddock would be "easy" in spite of the fact that Lasky's frame had been weakened considerably by illness. But they took their time about setting a new date with Braddock and stayed on the Coast for a longer spell than had been expected to watch a young Negro sensation out of Detroit who was being prominently mentioned for a shot with Lasky on the Coast. The young Negro's name was Joe Louis. On February 21st, 1935, this young Louis knocked Lee Ramage out in spectacular fashion in just two rounds at Los Angeles. Whether the quick knockout of Ramage had anything to do with it or not, only Lasky's handlers can say. The fact remains that they immediately forgot about a Louis fight and headed East to fight Braddock.

But Gould was still to have his headaches. With Lasky's return East, the Garden set Friday night, March 15th, as the date for the fight. Braddock began to train. About ten days before the 15th, however, Johnston called Gould on the 'phone and said that Lasky's managers had asked for an extra week to train and that the fight was being pushed over to March 22nd.

"What—another postponement?" roared Gould. But after expostulating at great length about the general injustice of things and what he considered a rank favoritism for Lasky on the Garden's part, he agreed to the 22nd, and informed Braddock to gait his training accordingly.

Two days later, however, he literally hit the ceiling when Johnston called him into the office and this time said that the fight was being pushed back to its original date—the 15th. Lasky, his managers had declared, would be ready after all.

"Is that so?" exploded Gould. "Well, they can go plumb to hell. What do they think this is, anyway? First, it's February 1st, and then he gets sick. Then it's March 15th, and then it's March 22nd, and now it's March 15th all over again. What do they think I've got here—a four-round fighter or something? Well, we WON'T fight on March 15th. We'll fight on March 22nd—and that's that."

With that, Gould stormed out of Johnston's office. As he bristled out, he shouted again, this time to the surprised Margie Regan, the mouth-open Sam McQuade, the rudely disturbed Albertanti, and all the rest, that he positively would not stand for another change in the date.

He hustled up to Stillman's gymnasium, instructed Braddock to train to fight on the 22nd, and then disappeared completely. Johnston had his men search all over the city for Gould. But Braddock's manager was not to be found. Finally, when it was too late to do anything else—and the fight was announced to the press by Johnston as definitely set for the 22nd—Gould reappeared in New York.

CHAPTER FOURTEEN

TWELVE AMAZING DAYS

MIKE JACOBS—
(HE DOES LOOK LIKE TEX)

IN THE twelve days which preceded the Lasky fight, some of the most amazing occurrences in the history of the ring unravelled themselves, one after the other, and paved the way for the installation of Jimmy Braddock as the man who would fight Max Baer for the World's heavyweight championship. Never before in the history of boxing had so many incidents, all having a distinct bearing on the nomination of a challenger for the heavyweight championship, occurred within so short a space of time.

Between the night of March 10th, 1935, and March 22nd, 1935, a period of only 12 days—but 288 hours—no less than FOUR men who had been rated ahead of Braddock as far as claims to first shot at Baer's crown were concerned—were by the queerest twists of fate eliminated from the picture and Braddock was left on the Garden's hands as the lone available contender.

The four men who were ahead of Braddock on March 10th, 1935, were Steve Hamas, Max Schmeling, Primo Carnera, and Art Lasky.

Steve Hamas, young Jersey heavyweight who, in his college days, had been a football star at Penn State, stood at the top of the list of challengers. In February, of the year before, Hamas had met Max Schmeling in Philadelphia and literally annihilated the Teuton, handing him a fearful beating even though Schmeling escaped being knocked out.

For a year or so, Hamas had been casting around since that victory, trying to cash in on it. But he and his manager, Charley Harvey (yes, the same Harvey who had managed Corn Griffin) had been getting the well-known "run-around."

Harvey visited the Garden day after day in an effort to get some recognition for his heavyweight-who needed action badly. He got the same answer on every visit. The Garden, he was repeatedly told, was really anxious to stage a return Hamas-Schmeling fight in New York, but Schmeling was unavailable right now, and Harvey would have to wait until later in the season.

Meanwhile, a report that the Garden had secretly come to an agreement with Joe Jacobs, Schmeling's manager, whereby Schmeling would be designated as the challenger for Baer's championship, regardless of how the "eliminations" turned out, proved anything but pleasant news to Harvey.

In the midst of all this, Walter Rothenburg, a German promoter, cabled Harvey an offer of $25,000 for Hamas to fight Schmeling in Germany. The offer was like manna from heaven to Harvey who had been waiting patiently for a year to hear such a proposition. It meant money in the bank at last, but before he cabled his acceptance, he informed the Garden of the offer and told Johnston that the Garden still could have the fight if it posted the $25,000 in five days.

For some inexplicable reason, however, the Garden neglected to post the $25,000 and Harvey and Hamas, feeling they were being tossed around again, slipped quietly out of New York harbor one day in February, on their way to Germany.

The trip ruined Steve Hamas' fistic career. Instead of licking Schmeling again and thereby strengthening his position as the chief challenger, Hamas, encountering an inspired Schmeling at a Nazi festival in Hamburg before some 30,000 persons on March 10th, took a fearful pummeling and finally was knocked out in the ninth round. He was so badly punished that he spent considerable time in a hospital following the bout.

Thus was he eliminated.

Schmeling, who conquered Hamas, eliminated himself. He wanted to fight Baer again—but he wanted to fight in Germany. Rothenburg now sent an offer of $300,000 to Baer to visit the Fatherland, and Schmeling, feeling that Baer hardly would dismiss such an offer, flatly refused to pay any attention to Jimmy Johnston's frantic cables from New York. He turned a deaf ear to Joe Jacobs, his manager, too.

Even if Baer did fight in New York in June, Schmeling was confident that the champion would win easily and then visit Germany in September to give him a shot at the title.

So Max decided to stay in the Fatherland.

Still very much in the picture at this time was Primo Carnera, from whom Baer had won the championship. The clamor for Carnera never reached the intensity of the one for Schmeling—but the Big Fellow from Sequals merited some consideration until the night of March 15th—only five days after the Schmeling-Hamas fight. On that night (the original date, incidentally, for the Braddock-Lasky rumpus) Carnera fought Big Ray Impellitiere in Madison Square Garden.

The battle of the behemoths, however, instead of providing an outstanding challenger, proved a dismal thing to watch and even though Carnera won, his stock following the fight was lower than it had been prior to the event. Not only that, but Carnera's managers, also hearing the story about the Garden secretly having come to an agreement with Schmeling and that the "eliminations" which were going on didn't mean a thing, decided to have a showdown. Louis Soresi, acting for Carnera, appeared at the Garden offices to demand a contract assuring his man of designation as the challenger for Baer's crown if Primo succeeded in surviving the eliminations. The Garden refused to give him any such contract, and Soresi, convinced that he was being taken for a "buggy-ride" marched down 49th street to the offices of Mike Jacobs, the Garden's rival, and signed a contract to fight Joe Louis for the Twentieth Century Sporting Club.

With Hamas and Carnera definitely out—and Schmeling exhibiting a marble-like indifference to all propositions, it was no wonder that Matchmaker Jimmy Johnston was hoping for a signal and overwhelming Lasky victory when the left-hooker from the Coast clambered through the ropes with James J. Braddock at Madison Square Garden on the night of March 22nd, 1935.

But Johnston was doomed to meet another jarring disappointment.

Instead of Lasky using Braddock as a springboard from which to plunge into the challenger's seat against Baer—the opposite came true.

Braddock won the Lasky fight decisively—and very easily, as compared to the Lewis fight. Perhaps Lasky did have a bad left hand. Perhaps the Coast star had not as yet recovered completely from the pleurisy which had laid him low some six weeks before. But the fact remains that Braddock licked him—and licked him by a tremendous margin.

A terrific right-hand punch to the nose into which Lasky ran shortly after the opening bell, played an immense role in bringing victory to the Jersey heavyweight.

Lasky had a habit of thrusting his jaw out at an opponent. Gould, Doc Robb, and Solly Seeman, the old lightweight, who were to work in Braddock's corner that night, had been informed of this tendency on Lasky's part. "The moment he sticks his chin out," they instructed Braddock, "let go with your right hand for all you're worth. He'll still be cold and you may catch him and ruin him for the night."

And an instant after the fight began, Braddock had landed. Lasky, thrusting his chin way out ahead of him, suddenly felt as though a sledge-hammer had struck him on the nose. The punch broke the nose and ruined Lasky's breathing for the night. Insofar as affecting the course of the fight, it was comparable to the famous punch which Tunney had landed on Dempsey in the first round of their first fight at Philadelphia.

Braddock then proceeded to win ten of the fifteen rounds. At every opportunity, he fired for the nose—and kept it stuffed with blood so regularly that Lasky had a desperate time of it breathing.

Winning the first round with that smashing and decisive wallop which he and his Board of Strategy had laid plans for before the fight, Braddock then galloped to the next two rounds as well. Lasky managed to take the fourth but lost the fifth because of a low punch. Braddock held him even in the sixth round, but in the seventh, Lasky enjoyed his best session of the fight, getting in close to Braddock and hooking solidly to earn the heat by a clear and overwhelming margin.

But if Lasky won the seventh by a big edge, Braddock took the eighth by an even bigger one. The Jerseyite drove Lasky all over the ring in this session with his terrific punches and the Garden was in a turmoil throughout. From that round on, Lasky weakened and Braddock grew stronger. From that round on, Lasky won only one more heat, the tenth, Braddock cracking his way to all the others with a steady stream of lefts to the head, interspersed whenever the opportunity offered with those jarring right hand smashes direct to Lasky's now highly abused nose.

The victory proved tremendously popular with the crowd of 10,000 which had turned out, for more reasons than one. Not only had Braddock been the underdog in the betting, but he also had been the much smaller man. Lasky had out-weighed him by almost 15 pounds, 182¼ against 197.

The New York Boxing Commission wasted no time in recognizing Braddock's sensational performance, either. The decision had hardly been announced when Commissioner Bill Brown informed the newspapermen at the ringside that Braddock would be "designated as the Number One Challenger for Baer's crown at the very next meeting of the commission."

CHAPTER FIFTEEN

HEAVYWEIGHT CHALLENGER AT LAST

EVEN Johnston was non-plussed at the unalterable determination of the commission to name Braddock as the Number One Challenger because the Jerseyite had survived the "eliminations." He explained to the commission that the Garden had conducted the eliminations "merely in fun," that nobody in the racket had taken them seriously and that he was positive Schmeling would come over from Germany to fight Baer.

But Johnston was wrong on Schmeling coming over—and the solons were insistent on Braddock as the challenger. On the 26th of March, at their regular Tuesday meeting, the boxing fathers named Braddock as the Number One Challenger for the heavyweight championship—but left a loophole for Schmeling to creep into the picture, if the German wanted to do so. "If he is sincere," announced the commission, "let him fight Braddock for the right to meet Baer."

In the midst of all this activity in New York, Baer, leaving Sacramento on March 27th for the East, and very much against Braddock as an opponent because he felt Braddock would not "draw"—fired a withering blast at the New York Commission.

"That (the naming of Braddock as the Number One Challenger) is the biggest laugh I've had in months," he told the *Associated Press*. "The New York Commission says Braddock is the Number One contender. And I suppose that makes it final. They call me a clown but I couldn't pull anything as funny as that if I sat up nights for a week."

"Why, five years ago, the New York Commission would not let me fight Braddock because they said he was a 'set up.' They insisted I meet a stronger opponent. Well, they gave me Ernie Schaaf, Tom Heeney and Tommy Loughran. I knocked Heeney out—but the other two beat me. Now they gallop up with Braddock and label him as the outstanding challenger for the title."

"I suppose this fellow Bill Brown is serious about supporting Braddock as the commission's leading contender. Well, my answer is that if Braddock is to fight me— let him lick my brother Buddy first. I think Buddy can beat him—and probably knock him right into Commissioner Brown's lap, too."

"There are three better challengers than Braddock. I don't think Braddock can stand up to Carnera, Schmeling or Joe Louis. I licked Carnera and Schmeling, and Louis' managers say he isn't ready to fight me yet. Let Braddock beat any one of those fellows and Commissioner Brown will have a leg to stand on."

"I am supposed to be only a dumb fighter, but if I cannot make better matches than the New York Commission, I'll go back to herding cows."

In view of subsequent occurrences, Baer's Sacramento oration made good reading. No doubt that Baer was dead serious about what he said. The champion openly preferred Schmeling for an opponent. "If Braddock needs money so badly, I'll let him be one of my sparring partners," he loftily announced on his way East. And at every whistle stop he paid his compliments to Bill Brown again and again. He had not forgotten how Brown, visiting Asbury the year before to watch him train for Carnera, had disgustedly told newspapermen, "why, this fellow seems to be training for the junior prom."

By the time Baer arrived in New York, his slaps and taunts at Braddock and Brown had gotten thoroughly under Joe Gould's skin. Baer threw a luncheon at Dempsey's restaurant, across the street from the Garden, the day he hit New York, and Gould, blood in his eye, headed for the place, Braddock with him.

Baer was seated at a table with his manager, Ancil Hoffman, Jack Dempsey, and several others as Gould and Braddock approached.

"Now tell Braddock to his face what you've been saying to the newspapermen on your way in," challenged Gould. Baer's answer disarmed both Gould and Braddock completely.

"Why, hel-lo, Jimmy," said Baer, jumping up, grasping and pumping Braddock's hand. "I'm glad you licked that Lasky fellow. He needed a licking. Congratulations."

Gould, who had come prepared for a riotous scene, was no end disconcerted by Baer's manner and congratulations. But he did not give up without a struggle.

"Is that all you've got to say to Jimmy?" he almost pathetically protested.

Baer just smiled—a big, wide Baer smile. "That's all," he replied.

"Well, all I can say is that you're a big phoney ——," hissed Gould.

Eventually they sat together, posed for pictures, ate some sandwiches and drank some beer. But when Baer walked out of the restaurant, he declared again that Braddock was not a suitable opponent because his manager was "too damn fresh." And Gould walked out saying to Jimmy, "Well, I told him something, anyway."

After several conferences with Johnston that failed to get anywhere, Baer and Hoffman headed westward for Chicago, where, on the night of April 12th, Buddy Baer fought in a preliminary to the Joe Louis-Roy Lazar card. Strange to relate, Buddy's foe that night was Corn Griffin, the same Griffin whom Braddock had knocked out in three rounds in June of 1934. Outweighing Corn almost 50 pounds (238½ to 189), Buddy broke Braddock's record for stopping Corn Griffin by a round: he stopped the southerner in two flat.

Baer and Hoffman were quick to seize a splendid talking point.

"There you are," boasted the champion. "What did I tell you? My brother knocks out in two rounds a fellow who went three rounds with Braddock. And they want Braddock to fight ME for the championship."

"Braddock just won't draw," protested Hoffman over and over again to Jimmy Johnston, who kept calling over the long-distance telephone. "Schmeling is the man to get, I tell you. He has just knocked out Steve Hamas and he is the best available opponent. Get him."

But Johnston had realized some time before that cabling Schmeling was a waste of both time and money. As a matter of fact, he had decided on April 11th that there was no sense fighting the New York Commission and that there was no keeping Braddock out of the challenger's spot. He finally came to terms with Gould four days before the April 15th deadline set by the contract with Baer for the naming of the challenger.

With Gould under contract, Johnston, on April 12th, formally informed the press that James J. Braddock, of North Bergen, N. J., had been designated as the challenger.

On April 13th, Braddock signed his contract which called for 17½ percent of the gate instead of the challenger's usual 15 percent, the extra percentage binding him to defend his title first for Madison Square Garden, if he defeated Baer.

And on April 16th, the New York Boxing Commission not only approved the match but set June 13th as the date.

Hoffman and Baer, however, still bristling with indignation, kept telegraphing and telephoning that Braddock was "not acceptable." Hoffman declared his contract with the Garden called for the Garden to name the "best available contender" and insisted that Braddock did not fit the requirements.

"We have been offered $300,000 to fight Schmeling in Germany," declared Hoffman. "Why should we fight Braddock in New York for peanuts? We'll go over there and collect the big money, that's what we'll do. Let the New York Commission suspend us. So what? When they name an opponent whom we figure will draw some money, then we'll return to New York to fight and the suspension will be lifted."

But two things occurred to change Hoffman's mind and eventually bring about the acceptance of Braddock.

First of all, the offer of $300,000 made by Walter Rothenburg, the German promoter, well enough as far as it went, didn't go far enough. Hoffman demanded the posting of certain sums in New York and London banks. Rothenburg must have been short of ready cash. Hoffman's demands were not complied with, sad to relate.

Still Hottman was turning a deaf ear to Johnston when Michael Strauss Jacobs, of the Twentieth Century Sporting Club, which for years had been trying to break the Garden's hold on heavyweight title fights, rushed from New York to Chicago to urge him to accept the Garden's offer and fight Braddock.

A strange thing for a Garden rival to do, of course. But Jacobs saw in the Braddock-Baer fight an opportunity to break at last the monopoly which the Garden had exercised over the promotion of heavyweight championship fights for years.

By virtue of that tiny but highly important clause inserted in all contracts drawn up with challengers for the heavyweight title, requiring the challengers, in the event they dethroned the champion, to engage in one fight under the auspices of the Garden before they fought for anybody else, the corporation had been able to keep a firm hand on all heavyweight title promotions.

"Here's our chance to get those championship fights away from the Garden," the Twentieth Century representatives said to Hoffman. "Grab this fight. Braddock will be easy for your man. And once the fight is over, you become your own boss. You'll be able to fight whom you please and for whom you please. You'll be able to dictate your own terms as champion. We've got Carnera and Louis signed to fight on June 28th. Forget about that European trip and Schmeling; you'd be crazy to go over there and risk your title. Go through with the Braddock fight for the Garden here in New York. Maybe that match won't draw a million. But you can come right back into New York again in September for us and fight the Louis-Carnera winner and you ought to get at least $400,000 for your end, for there's a fight that will surely gross a million."

Louis and Carnera at the time loomed as easy targets in Hoffman's eye. And so, after such a telling argument delivered by the Garden's most bitter rival, he finally decided he would take Braddock. But before he capitulated to the Garden, he shrewdly squeezed something else out of Johnston. He forced Johnston to turn over to Baer the exclusive radio rights for the fight as well as the champion's end of the purse. Then—and only then—did Baer and Hoffman agree to fight Jersey Jim.

CHAPTER SIXTEEN

CAMP IS PITCHED AT LOCH SHELDRAKE

WITH Braddock finally set for the fight—and Johnston (who by this time nightly was consigning Baer and Hoffman to a certain place more popular for its company than its temperature), thumping the ballyhoo drums for all he was worth, declaring Baer was "the worst champion we ever had," and that Braddock would beat him, too, just as surely as he had beaten Lasky, Lewis and Corn Griffin, little Joe Gould laid his plans.

He decided that Baer, who simply refused to take Braddock seriously, would not be prepared for a long, tough fight. He felt that Baer would be dangerous only in the first three or four rounds—and that once the fight got past those early rounds, condition would tell. He knew that Baer had been burning the candle at both ends, and the reports he received of Baer's rather mediocre showing against Eddie Simms in an exhibition at Cleveland just after Braddock had finally been accepted as the challenger, made him more convinced than ever that the champion never would be in shape for a drawn-out, grueling struggle. Not only that, but Baer was reported to have injured his hand, too, in the Simms exhibition.

"Say, maybe he'll break it completely the first time he hits Braddock," said Gould gleefully, "and then we'll just coast in."

To the end of conditioning Braddock for fifteen rounds of the most vicious kind of fighting, Gould dedicated himself. Over and over again, he repeated to newspapermen, "If the fight goes 15 rounds—Baer will collapse. Condition will win for us. I'm going to toughen that Braddock up like he's never been toughened before. What a surprise we're going to give that Baer."

He chose a magnificent site for Braddock's training camp. Deep into the Catskills he cut, and one day came the announcement that Loch Sheldrake—a beautiful spot in the mountain country, some 1800 feet above sea level—had been chosen. The camp was a trifle over 100 miles from New York City and was pitched on the property of the Hotel Evans.

Braddock reported to camp on April 27th—seven weeks before the fight.

For two weeks, neither newspapermen, nor seconds, nor sparring partners bothered him. For two weeks, he lived the life of a hermit. For two weeks he roamed the mountainside by himself, running five or six miles every morning, delving into the forests later in the day, axe on shoulder, to hack away at trees, and crawling between the sheets at an early hour each night.

Those two weeks made a changed man out of Jimmy Braddock.

The starving stevedore, who had been on hash for a year, and who had been forced to miss more meals in the preceding two years than he cared to remember, had since the Lasky fight, been eating regularly. But he only started to REALLY eat when he hit Sheldrake. Lamb chops, steaks, vegetables, chicken, roast duck—all roared pell-mell down Jimmy's gullet. He ate well and he slept well. Nobody bothered him and he bothered nobody. His hosts, Ike and Art Evans, saw to that.

When, at the end of those two weeks, his faithful trainer, Doc Robb, accompanied by Francis Albertanti, who was to be the camp's press agent, appeared on the scene, Braddock actually was a changed man. The tape revealed some startling figures. Braddock, a slow-maturing Irishman, had undergone a most amazing transformation.

Unbelievable though it may sound, Braddock had, since the Lasky fight, grown a full inch and now stood six feet, three inches in altitude. And his body which had displaced 182 and a fraction pounds for the Lasky fight—now weighed almost 220 pounds!

No one believed the initial stories that poured out of Sheldrake, concerning the amazing change in Braddock. Only those who visited the camp and saw for themselves realized that press agent Francis Albertanti was not letting his mimeograph run away with him. The answer to the strange physical phenomenon simply was that Braddock had been clamoring for two years for maturity—but did not attain it until more prosperous circumstances enabled him to give his growing system what it required.

Fight camps have ever had distinguishing aspects. So did this one. From the day that Joe Gould, accompanied by a flock of sparring partners, joined Braddock, Robb and Albertanti, the attitude at Loch Sheldrake was, "What have we got to lose?"

There was hilarity about that camp, always. And thankfulness, too. Every time Albertanti sat down to breakfast, lunch or supper, he would murmur a thanks to Corn Griffin. "We'd never have been here," he remarked day after day, "if it hadn't been for good old Corn."

Gould loudly echoed Albertanti's sentiments.

The first thing Albertanti did upon his arrival at camp was to cross-examine Braddock for an entire afternoon. The Jerseyite never was a talkative type, but Albertanti's constant attack finally got results. "jeepers, come on," Francis would plead, "I've got to get your history together."

Eventually Albertanti finished his questioning and Braddock sat wearily down to supper while Albertanti sat down to celebrate. And how he celebrated! But he was up very bright and early the next morning and aside from stopping to answer half a dozen phone calls during the day— he did not leave his typewriter in the press room until he had banged out a 16-page history of Braddock which was then mimeographed and the next day mailed out to sportswriters the country over as the first broadside out of Sheldrake.

Seven out of ten telephone conversations at that camp were with Jimmy Johnston, who called at any and all times from his office in New York. The author listened in on many of those calls and on several occasions substituted for Albertanti, who every so often became completely worn out repeating over and over again the same old answers to the same old questions.

"———————— ——," he would moan as the phone rang. "There's that Johnston again. He talked to me only half an hour ago. I suppose he now wants to know what Braddock did in the last half hour."

He would pick up the telephone.

"Hello," Johnston would start, "Albertanti? How'd he look today."

"He looked good."

"He looked good? Why did he look good?"

"Well, because he looked good. Don't I know when a fighter looks good?"

"How many rounds did he box?"

"He boxed six rounds."

"Only six rounds. Why did he box only six rounds?"

"I don't know why he boxed only six rounds. You'll have to ask Gould."

"Well, tell Gould I said he should box eight rounds."

"Yes, I'll tell him."

(Gould, usually listening in, would snort.)

"Was he on the road this morning?"

"Yes, he was on the road this morning."

"How many miles did he run?"

"I don't know."

"You don't know? Didn't you get up and check on him?"

"No—I have to get SOME sleep————"

"Well, find out how many miles he ran today."

"Gould says he ran seven miles."

"Only seven miles? He should run ten miles every morning. Tell Gould ————"

At this point, a low moan would emanate from Albertanti.

One day, Gould, anxious to use the telephone himself for a call, and irritated beyond end as Johnston fired instructions to have this and that done, exploded.

"Tell Johnston," he roared, "that Gould says that he has been managing Braddock for ten years now and that he says for Johnston to mind his own damn business and to stop worrying Gould about Braddock. After all these years, I should know what to do—and I am not going to let Johnston tell me how to handle my fighter."

"Gould says," began Francis. But he got no further.

"Is that so?" Johnston, who had heard the roaring, fired back. "Well, tell Gould that I say———"

And so on. Sometimes five and six times a day.

Yes, in many respects, this was a "screwy" camp as one writer put it. Braddock, unlike most fighters who dislike being interviewed and questioned day after day by newly arriving members of the press— literally lived in the press room and always was available for anything that was required.

Years before, at Saratoga, where he had trained for his fight with Tommy Loughran, he had been the same way. On many a night he had helped Norman St. Denis, son of Walter St. Denis, stamp and mail the daily publicity out of camp. He sat down often and did likewise at Loch Sheldrake in 1935. Now and then he played "hearts" with a few of the boys. On other occasions he just hung around and watched the nightly poker or pinochle game. Very frequently, after eating, he spread himself upon the couch outside the press room, where he chinned with the boys. Or, when he felt like it, he went for a short walk with Mrs. Braddock, who added to the novelty of this most odd of all odd fight camps, by remaining throughout the training grind.

He was always available to newspapermen, photographers and the army of autograph seekers, even though Jack McCarthy, one of his sparmates, several times was introduced as Braddock to the latter group and obliged by signing Jimmy's name on postal cards, dollar bills, handkerchiefs and what not.

CHAPTER SEVENTEEN

THE RELIEF STORY BREAKS IN THE NEWSPAPERS

HARDLY had Braddock become established in his quarters at Loch Sheldrake when a particularly hot political fight in his home town of North Bergen brought to light the fact that the man who was going to fight Baer for the world's heavyweight championship had been on relief for the greater part of the year preceding his climb to the title bout.

Struggling for political control of North Bergen township in May, 1935, were Paul F. Cullum, who was to win the struggle and who is now mayor of North Bergen, and Julius L. Reich, who was mayor then. In the midst of a speech during which he was roundly assailing his foes, Reich one night charged that "a man who is going to soon fight for the world's heavyweight championship is still on our township's relief rolls."

Intended as a smashing blow at the Cullum forces, the charge, which was inaccurate in that Braddock had been off relief since the Lasky fight, not only reacted as a boomerang against Reich—but in addition hurled the hitherto somewhat neglected Braddock-Baer fight right onto Page One in the newspapers.

Despite the fierce intensity with which Jimmy Johnston had insisted Braddock would fool everybody and hand Baer the surprise of his life, the fight was getting scant attention in the newspapers. The boxing writers themselves generally felt that the match was too one-sided. And Baer's countless broadsides from the very beginning, repeated at regular intervals even after he started training, that Braddock was a joke challenger, enhanced this feeling. Even Ancil Hoffman ridiculed Braddock. "They better have an ambulance ready for him," he said one day, showing a remarkable concern for the challenger's welfare.

The general attitude towards the fight was expressed succinctly by Lawrence Perry, veteran sports commentator, in a syndicated article which appeared in the newspapers on April 16th. Perry wrote "no one seems to care whether our terpsichorean champion meets the Jersey longshoreman or not."

Yet in the very same article, Perry also remarked "a Baer-Braddock go might not be half so bad as it looks. The champion has not been taking the best care of himself and if by hook or crook the Jerseyman could weather seven rounds of cyclonic haymakers—a rather doubtful contingency, it must be confessed—the jazz champ might find himself facing a lot of real trouble."

The fact remains, however, that at the time the fight finally was closed, interest in it was scarce, if not almost nil.

But within two weeks, newspapers throughout the country suddenly began printing all kinds of stories about Braddock—and, of course, the fight. A press agent couldn't have engineered things better.

After all, it was not every day that a heavyweight, especially one who was married and the father of three children, came off relief rolls to fight for the championship of the world.

The New York dailies, hitherto all but ignoring Braddock, suddenly put the "family man" challenger on Page One. "Case 2796" (which incidentally, was not the correct number) became famous. Pictures soon appeared of Jimmy's family, his wife, and his three darling children, Jay, Howard and baby Rose Marie. Not only did the American newspapers go for the story in a big way, but so, too, did publications abroad. The London *Daily Express* featured Jimmy Braddock on Page One, and its famous boxing expert, Trevor Wignall, began to make preparations to go across the ocean to cover the fight. There was after all something decidedly extraordinary to this championship bout.

The election in North Bergen, which had been responsible for the revelations, made the headlines in the New York newspapers, too. Soon, Reich, who had made the charge, found he had made a ghastly error. His opponents had fired viciously back at him, pronounced him grossly inaccurate, pointed out that Braddock had gone off relief with the Lasky fight and then censured him roundly for citing an individual's personal misfortunes as campaign fodder. The general public also seemed to feel that Reich had been guilty of a breach of etiquette disgraceful even for a politician, and on Election Day, May 14th, he suffered a thundering defeat at the polls.

Braddock stayed up past his usual ten o'clock bedtime the night of the 14th at Loch Sheldrake, just to find out who had won the election. At 10:30 p. m., Gould put in a long-distance call to the *Hudson Dispatch* and asked for "sports." The author answered the phone.

"This is Joe Gould calling from Loch Sheldrake," Gould announced. "Jimmy can't go to sleep. He wants to know who won the election in North Bergen."

"Tell him Cullum and Buesser ran away with it."

"Good," the author could hear Jimmy exclaim, "I'm glad my friends won."

"He's going to bed now," said Gould.

"How does he feel about the relief business coming out?" the author asked.

"Well, he doesn't like it, of course," said Gould. "But it's out now—and what can he do about it? It has made him more determined than ever to win the 13th, however, so he won't ever have to go on relief again," he concluded.

Naturally, Braddock never forgave Reich for making the disclosures. But the cold facts are that Reich actually did not only Braddock but everybody else connected with the fight, a tremendous favor when he made his charges.

The relief angle rescued what otherwise might have been a terrific financial flop. As it was, the Garden, it was reported, cleared some forty thousand dollars on the promotion. The tussle, when it finally came off, drew a little over $205,000—not a tremendous fistic gate by any means, but a bit better anyway than the 1933 Sharkey-Carnera championship gate of $198,000. Judging by the manner in which Braddock was being ridiculed as the "weakest challenger in history," it might not have drawn even $150,000—but for the relief revelations. Thousands who went to the fight that night in June went simply to root for Braddock, the family man with the three kids who had been on relief. They felt he had no chance, but they were going to root for him, anyway—and if by some twist of fate he did score the biggest of all upsets and win—they wanted to be witnesses to the miracle.

An arresting indication as to just how the relief angle affected interest in the fight was given on Thursday evening, June 20th, one week after

Braddock had won the title, at a dinner tendered him as the new champion at the St. Moritz Hotel, in New York City.

Chunky Fiorello H. LaGuardia, mayor of New York, rose to speak:

"You cannot imagine how interested the general public was in your fight," LaGuardia declared, looking directly at Jimmy. "The story of how you were on relief and fought your way to the championship for your wife and three kids did more for boxing than any fight in the last twenty-five years.

"Why," exclaimed the mayor with a smile, "the first thing my wife asked me at the breakfast table the morning after the fight was: 'Well, did the three kids win?' "

CHAPTER EIGHTEEN

MURDERERS' ROW

JACK
McCARTHY

THE relief story had just spread itself across the newspapers when Gould arrived at camp with a quartet of sturdy-looking sparring partners. They were Paul Pross, a rugged German, who had been born, the day his father died in a trench in France, Norman Barnett, a former University of Maryland fullback, Jack McCarthy, a beefy Bostonian who had worked for some years as a sparmate for Jack Sharkey, and Don Petrin, of New Jersey, who had gained considerable publicity in 1930 when dismissed from Max Schmeling's Endicott camp for making the German look crude. Pross weighed 210 pounds, Barnett was around 205, McCarthy scaled about 192, and Petrin, the speed artist, was 185. Together they formed the best set of sparring partners to prepare a heavyweight since Dempsey's days.

In the weeks to follow, the four men mentioned above proved themselves splendid conditioners for the champion. Not only did they take punishment, but they dealt it out, too. As a matter of fact, the workouts at Loch Sheldrake became such furious punching bees that newspapermen, who began filtering in and out of camp after the 15th of

May, wondered at times whether the challenger and his manager had not gone a bit daffy.

For every afternoon, what did Braddock do but get out there and actually FIGHT five or six or seven or eight rounds with his sparring partners. And the sessions were all crowded with dynamite. Braddock held nothing back; his partners did likewise. It was by far the most unorthodox fight camp the scribes had seen in years.

While Baer, down at Asbury, clowned around the greater part of each round, Braddock, at Loch Sheldrake, slugged and was slugged for fully three minutes of each round. And just to intensify this butchery, Gould had ordered Doc Robb to alternate Braddock's sparring partners so that a fresh man faced Jimmy in every round. If Petrin boxed the first round, Pross went in for the second, Barnett for the third, and McCarthy for the fourth. And then Petrin started all over again. This routine was repeated day after day.

It is only fair to say that Braddock was not particularly impressive in his early workouts. Through those early sessions, he was hit hard and often by right-hand punches—Baer's favorite smash. Pross and McCarthy connected regularly with right handers. Following a particular workout, one newspaperman reported that Braddock had been hit "fifty times on the lug in eight rounds."

But there was a method in Joe Gould's madness. Braddock was definitely being groomed to withstand right-hand punches.

Never did Gould permit a let-up.

"We'll get this fellow in shape like he's never been in before," he said as he watched the boys slam away at one another. "Suppose Baer does knock this guy down. Do you think he's going to stay down? You're crazy. You can go and bet your shirt that Braddock will get up—and when he gets up, he is a hard man to handle. Remember Corn Griffin."

On another afternoon when the punching in the ring reached astounding proportions, he literally shrieked with delight.

Turning finally to Murray Robinson, of the Newark *Star Eagle*, who was nearby, he shouted:

"Look at Braddock! Look at Braddock, will you! Say—he is going to be in wonderful shape—IF HE LIVES!"

Things reached such a point that Jack Miley, of the New York *Daily News*, date-lined his stories out of Sheldrake "Homicide Hall." Paul Gallico, also of the *News*, wrote:

"James J. has the roughest crew of spar boys ever assembled at any heavyweights training camp, and from 4 to 4:45 every afternoon, he amuses himself by prizefighting with them. And when I say prizefighting, that is also what I mean. For this business that goes on by the bonnie banks of Loch Sheldrake can by no stretch of the imagination be called sparring. It is fighting pure and simple. It is really the screwiest training camp you ever saw. Braddock has four big, strong guys, all of whom can fight, and he stays in there for six rounds and fights them while Joe Gould, his manager, sits back on his haunches and rocks with glee. 'Is that something? . . . Is that a fight? . . . Look at 'em fighting,' says Mr. Gould, while blows thud off the skulls of challenger and hired hands alike."

No wonder Braddock's training camp soon became known as "Murderers' Row."

Although Murderers' Row all but made Joe Gould's heart stop ticking on more than one occasion, the challenger's condition became more and more impressive as the days rolled into weeks. Unfortunately, the boxing writers, concentrating on the Jimmy McLarnin-Barney Ross fight around this time, failed to get a good line on Braddock. Had they watched his workouts steadily, no doubt more than just a handful would have conceded him a chance to upset the dope and beat Baer.

As it was, the newspapermen were watching Ross work at Ferndale, some ten miles away, and McLarnin at Swan Lake, also in the vicinity. Nobody had time to bother with Loch Sheldrake. just four days before the McLarnin-Ross fight, however, Joe Gould thanked his stars that Sheldrake was devoid of newspapermen.

It was Friday night, May 24th. Gould was playing poker in the pressroom with Ike and Art Evans, Lou Kaminsky, telegraph operator, and an old gentleman with a goatee named Pa Blumenstein.

Braddock and Doc Robb had just gone upstairs to hit the hay.

They had not been gone any more than ten minutes when Robb reappeared in the doorway. As Gould looked up in surprise, Robb excitedly motioned for him to leave the poker game.

Gould left the table at once. The expression on Robb's face had startled him.

When he got upstairs, he found Braddock in bed-holding his left side, apparently in agony.

"What's happened?" exclaimed Gould, Visioning a fall down the stairs or some other such misfortune.

"I can't breathe," replied Jimmy slowly. "One of those shots . . . in the ribs . . . here . . . this afternoon . . . it hurt at the time . . . but I thought the pain would go away. But it . . . hasn't. And now I can't breathe. It feels like . . . the rib is broken."

Globes of sweat popped on Gould's brow.

"Shut that door," he snapped at Robb. But Robb, hard of hearing, did nothing of the kind. Gould looked up, noted the door was still open, and carefully shut it himself.

For a moment, there was silence.

"We're ruined if the papers get wind of this," Gould remarked gloomily. He turned around to Robb.

"Go down and get Albertanti."

Albertanti, also startled, came puffing up the stairs.

A short conference was held. It was decided to rush Jimmy in the middle of the night to his physician back in Hudson County.

"There are no newspapermen in camp now," said Gould. "They're all covering Ross and McLarnin. But some of them may drop in here tomorrow. If they do, tell them Braddock got a hurry call and went to town. Tell them his mother was sick. Don't breathe a word of this—understand."

Robb helped Braddock dress as Gould went downstairs to get a car ready for the trip to Jersey. Fifteen minutes later they were on their way—Gould and Braddock sitting in the back of the car, Solly Seeman driving. It was a long, silent, miserable drive.

153

Thoughts of all sorts flashed through Gould's mind—and Jimmy's mind, too. They had been waiting, dreaming, hoping, praying for years for a shot at the heavyweight title. Now that they had finally landed one, things sure were going wrong. The Ross-McLarnin struggle and the Joe Louis-Primo Carnera fight (which was to go on after the Braddock-Baer shindig) were stealing the spotlight away from the championship bout as it was. And, on top of that, if Braddock found it necessary to request a postponement because of an injury inflicted by one of his sparmates . . . well, it would ruin the fight completely. But what else was there to be done—if the rib was broken?

It was almost two o'clock in the morning when the midnight riders reached the office of Dr. M. J. McDonnell, in North Bergen. Cautiously peering up and down the dark street, to make sure no late passers-by were around, the fighter, his manager, and Solly the second, mounted the steps and rang the doorbell.

They were ushered into the waiting room. The doctor was first sworn to secrecy, and then proceeded to make his examination.

Gould was ashen gray when the doctor pronounced his findings. So was Solly Seeman.

"He has a badly dented rib," explained the doctor, "and some of the muscles underneath the rib are torn."

Gould finally recovered enough voice to ask hollowly:

"How long will it take to heal up?"

"Well, maybe nine or ten days," replied the doctor. "But he will have to lay off boxing entirely for that period. And he also will have to protect the damaged side with some kind of a brace."

"Please, Doc, don't say a word about it to anybody, please," begged Gould. "And make up a regular doctor's report for me, just in case I have to ask for a postponement."

The doctor placed Braddock under diathermic treatment as Gould and Seeman, the world toppling about their ears, looked on. Dr. McDonnell then wrote out his report. It was around half past three in the morning when Braddock, Gould and Seeman left the doctor's office. There was a momentary halt on the steps.

"Back to camp?" asked Seeman.

"No, we won't go back to camp," Gould said, after several moments of heavy thinking. "We'll go across the river to my home in New York. That testimonial dinner for Jimmy at the Union City Elks Club is Sunday night, anyway. We can say we came into town for that. We'll go back to camp Monday and see how you feel by then," he announced, looking at Braddock. "We won't ask for a postponement unless we absolutely have to."

"But how are we going to keep the sportswriters from finding out?" asked Seeman. "If Jim doesn't box for ten days, they're bound to suspect something is wrong."

"Come on, get going," said Gould, "we're not going to worry about that now."

They bundled into the car and drove to Gould's apartment in New York City, where Braddock rested all of Saturday and most of Sunday, too.

While Braddock rested in New York City, Albertanti held the fort at Loch Sheldrake. Fortunately for him, the newspapermen stayed away from Sheldrake in droves. Only one sportswriter was interested enough to appear at Braddock's camp for Saturday's scheduled workout; he was the author, who had driven a hundred miles to see Jim in action and to discuss with Gould and Jim some of the details of the dinner which was to be held on Sunday night.

Informed by Albertanti that Braddock had gone home during the night because of a "telephone call that his mother was sick"—this lone newspaperman decided (to Albertanti's great relief) to stifle his disappointment at Braddock's absence by hurrying to Ferndale, eight miles away, to see Barney Ross drill.

On Sunday, the camp's publicity general had an even easier time of it. That day, no one at all disturbed the tranquility of the Sheldrake Sabbath and Albertanti spent the afternoon on the porch, smoking. Only a few miles away, the army of boxing writers first watched Ross drill and then, piling into automobiles, hustled over to McLarnin's camp and watched the champion step through his finishing paces. Most of the writers then headed for home, some to write their concluding articles at their various offices, others to attend the Braddock Testimonial Dinner in Union City.

Despite a series of terrific obstacles which the committee in charge will remember for some time, the dinner for Braddock turned out to be a riotous success. Close to 1200 persons, practically double the capacity of the modestly-sized Elks Club, flooded the building top and bottom to pay tribute to New Jersey's first heavyweight title challenger. So many crowded into the place, that the affair became unwieldy. The caterer did his little bit to add to the general confusion by refusing to serve the dinner (after first whetting the appetites of the hungry 1200 by pushing out the initial course) until he was paid so much money in advance. For a protracted spell (over an hour) caterer and various members of the committee were locked in a huddle. Finally, Mayor Paul F. Cullum, of North Bergen, and Joe Gould, hearing what was up, went to the rescue of committee members Pat Sullivan and Henry Moser, who were waging a losing battle with the caterer. Checks were written—and the crowd in the ballroom, now in a state of high merriment thanks to a plenitude of something else in the absence of food, got its dinner at last.

The dinner menu had been printed in green—and the caption beneath the cartoon of Braddock on the front cover read: "James J. Braddock, next heavyweight champion of the world."

The Braddock Boosters, who were staging the dinner, certainly had confidence in their hero, even if they had run a little short of cash.

It was at this dinner that Braddock, the "Forgotten Man," suddenly realized that he had well-wishers, hundreds and hundreds and hundreds of them.

Jack Dempsey, his early idol, was among the first speakers introduced by Toastmaster Jackie Farrell. Dempsey wished Braddock luck but refused to pick a winner. Because of another engagement, Dempsey then hurried away. What the newspapers fondly call "a distinguished array of fistic and political lights" followed the former heavyweight champion in showering plaudits and well wishes upon Braddock.

Jimmy Johnston, of Madison Square Garden, told how he had given Braddock the Griffin, Lewis and Lasky fights in succession, hoping "to get rid of" Braddock in that fashion, and how Braddock had crossed him each time. Then, very seriously, Johnston told the audience that Braddock positively would lick Baer. "If he is in good condition," declared Johnston, "he will knock Baer's head off." He looked squarely at Braddock as he said that, little dreaming that Braddock was suffering at the time from a badly bruised rib which three persons in the room very dolefully feared would bring about a request for a postponement of the fight. Johnston probably would have collapsed had he known how Braddock's side was taped up.

Philadelphia Jack O'Brien, after taking a choice rap at the tardiness of the waiters in serving the dinner, warned Braddock that he had a tough road ahead of him. No less than three United States Congressmen paid the challenger their respects and expressed the belief that he would bring the world's heavyweight championship to New Jersey for the first time. From Gene Tunney, the retired undefeated heavyweight champion, came an inspiring telegram telling Braddock that "confidence in one's self" was a tremendous factor in boxing as in anything else.

Late in the night, Jim's father, a massive figure of a man, with snow-white hair and features that reminded one of John L. Sullivan, delivered in a thick Irish brogue that seemed to come from Donnelly's Hollow itself, perhaps the best speech of the night.

"It was a damned decent night," he said. "You have paid my boy a fine tribute. May the best man win."

And only a few feet away from the center of the dais where her son was seated, sat Mrs. Elizabeth O'Toole Braddock, Jimmy's mother, not at all sick, nor even aware her health had been trifled with to keep newspapermen from sensing that her son had suffered a rib injury.

"How do you feel, Mrs. Braddock?" one scribe inquired of her during the night.

"Oh, she didn't feel so well this morning," hastily explained Joe Gould, "but she wouldn't have missed Jim's dinner for anything."

And he hurried her away.

It was almost half past twelve when judge Robert V. Kinkead, final speaker of the night, concluded the dinner with a vivid, inspiring address, in which he reiterated the faith that Hudson County had in Braddock and predicted that Jimmy would bring the world's heavyweight title to Hudson County. He presented the guest of honor with a wrist watch on behalf of the gathering.

Braddock made a very short speech of acceptance, mumbling something about not desiring to "murder" his audience with words. A few minutes later Gould had spirited him out of the building.

"Come," he said, "we are going back to camp right now. We won't wait until tomorrow."

The ride back to Loch Sheldrake was another silent one. Both Gould and Braddock were thinking of the torn rib muscles—and also the astonishing spirit which had prevailed at the dinner. There had been such a bubbling air of friendship and faith and hope that Murray Robinson, of the Newark *Star Eagle*, wrote the next day:

"It was the most impressive, spontaneous tribute ever paid to a fighter. It was friendly and fraternal and free from the synthetic, publicity-grabbing air which usually permeates such gatherings.

"Baer's dinner (held around the same time) stood out in sharp contrast . . . there was no personal bond between the Californian and the merrymakers. They came chiefly because they wanted to get a closeup of the Livermore Lothario and because the party was thrown at a very nice spot. The Braddock testimonial, on the other hand, was attended by Braddock's neighbors and friends . . . who flocked to the banquet hall to show him that they were with him. Those present knew Braddock personally."

Truer words were never written.

It was almost four o'clock in the morning when Braddock and Gould arrived back at Sheldrake.

"How do you feel now, Jim?" asked Joe as they got out of the car.

"I'll be all right," replied Braddock grimly. "I'd die if I ever had to disappoint the mob that was at the Elks Club."

But as they went to bed, both wondered how Jimmy was going to keep his injury from sportswriters who, they felt certain, would pour into camp the next day.

Call it Luck, call it Fate, call it Destiny, call it what you will—but not only the next day—but actually for the next six days not a sports writer appeared at Braddock's camp!

It was simply another of the uncanny occurrences which were to mark Braddock's march to the world's heavyweight championship.

Ordinarily, sports writers would have flocked in by the two and threes, some to stay for just one workout, some to stay several days, some to stay perhaps a week. Had they appeared thus at camp, it might have become urgently necessary for Mrs. Elizabeth O'Toole Braddock to suffer a recurrence of the obliging "malady" which had "forced" her son to leave camp so suddenly and mysteriously the Friday night before.

But from Monday, May 27th, to Saturday, June 1st, Braddock's camp was No Man's Land as far as newspapermen were concerned.

The Ross-McLarnin fight was, of course, responsible for their absence.

Ross and McLarnin staged their final boxing drills on Saturday, May 25th, and Sunday, May 26th. The sportswriters, naturally, sat in on those concluding workouts. And when Ross and McLarnin broke camp to head for New York—the sportswriters did likewise.

They were in New York on Monday, May 27th, and Tuesday, May 28th, on which date the Ross-McLarnin shindig took place. The fates were kind to Braddock the night of the fight, too. Ross was given the verdict after a particularly close scrap and the howls that went up about the decision kept the sportswriters busy for several days. Pop Foster, McLarnin's manager, cried to the heavens that his Jimmy had been jobbed out of a championship. He charged malfeasance, nonfeasance, misfeasance and what not. His vehement declarations got him into trouble and before Pop showed the proper humility towards the boxing fathers to bring the row to an end, the week was practically up.

When the boxing writers finally did wash their hands of McLarnin and Ross, they first turned towards Asbury Park to watch Baer, the champion. And by the time they did begin to float into Sheldrake, it was Saturday and Braddock was ready to box again.

161

8

Gould took no chances when Braddock resumed boxing. A special leather protector was strapped around Jimmy's ribs and he wore it until all pain had disappeared. To hide this protector Braddock always pulled on two heavy sweatshirts and kept them on throughout his drills. On one broiling Sunday afternoon in particular, when a blistering sun was inducing a flood of perspiration that just poured from Jimmy's face and legs, no one could fathom why Gould insisted on Braddock wearing two sweatshirts, a white one underneath, a green one on top.

And for obvious reasons, Gould wouldn't tell why.

The newspapermen who did appear at Braddock's camp for the last week of training, were amazed.

Braddock's size, his left hand, his boxing ability, his calmness and confidence surprised the scribes. Ed Van Every wrote in the New York *Sun* on June 5th that Braddock's "confidence in himself was absolute as Tunney's on the eve of his first battle with Dempsey. The mood of the two under similar conditions is almost identical."

Particularly surprised were the newspapermen who had first visited Baer's camp and who were getting their first glimpse of the challenger afterwards. The reaction of Trevor Wignall, the famous English authority, was typical. Wignall was plainly startled.

"Why," he remarked as Jimmy rattled a steady fire of lefts into Paul Pross' face, "this fellow is a good boxer. I never thought he could move like that. When the story (that Braddock had been named the challenger) hit England, our impression was that he was a clumsy, slow-footed heavyweight whose right-hand punch was his lone stock in trade."

On the same day (June 6th) that Wignall visited Braddock's camp, a ruddy-faced Irishman named Bill Brown also was present. Brown watched Braddock very closely. When the workout ended, the newspapermen pressed the Commissioner for a statement.

"As far as physical condition is concerned," Brown said, "Braddock is in excellent shape. He is in far better shape than when I saw him ten days ago. But he is a little open for a right-hand punch," concluded the Commissioner. "He will have to tighten his defense."

"If Brown thinks he is in good condition—that's all I want to know," declared Gould. "Baer won't be able to hit Braddock with a right. Jimmy knows how to avoid that. It's condition that is going to win this fight."

The next day, June 7th, was Braddock's 29th birthday. Obviously pleased with Jimmy's condition, and guarding against overtraining, Gould decided to give the challenger a day off.

"There won't be any workout today," he said. "Take it easy."

Some hours later, however, Gould was walking about the grounds of the hotel with several newspapermen, discussing the fight, when he noticed a commotion near the arena in which the outdoor ring was pitched. Marching over to see what was up, he was stumped to find Braddock in the ring, shadow boxing.

While Gould looked on in amazement, Braddock stepped eight rounds in all, skipping rope, shadow boxing, doing some calisthenics and then punching the light and heavy bags for a spell.

"Maybe I'm crazy," said Joe, when it was over, "but I thought this was to be a day off. Maybe you'll tell me what it's all about."

"Oh, I just got a little ambitious," grinned Braddock as he hustled for the showers.

"That's his idea of a day off," Gould turned to the newspapermen. "Eight rounds of work. Boy, he's going to be in shape for that Baer!"

Jimmy's finishing drills were held on Saturday, June 8th, and Sunday, June 9th. They were by far his best exhibitions. But as luck would have it, the heaviest kind of a downpour drenched the countryside over the week end and made the final drills more or less private affairs.

Only four newspapermen were in camp for those last two workouts. They were Hugh Bradley, sports editor of the New York *Evening Post*, Fred Van Ness, of the *New York Times*, Caswell Adams, of the New York *Tribune*, and the writer. A group consisting of Edward J. Niel, of the *Associated Press*, Al Buck, of the New York *Post*, Jack Miley, of the New York *Daily News*, and Joe Nichols, of the *New York Times*, had left Braddock's camp Friday night to finish up with Baer at Asbury. No doubt, had the weather been more agreeable, Braddock's final drills would have seen more newspaper representation at the ringside—but as it was, only the four scribes were present.

Braddock never punched harder than he did in those last drills. On Saturday afternoon, he punished his sparmates severely, boxed well, and indicated he was quite able to avoid a right-hand punch when he wanted to do so by circling gracefully away from the other fellow's right hand and jabbing solidly with his left as he did.

Saturday night, he gave evidence that he had just about reached edge. Perhaps the steady rain, dampening everything in the mountains, had something to do with his crankiness. He stopped speaking to everybody, and his wife, Mae, explained that it was a sure sign he was ready to go.

Before retiring, however, Braddock did utter a few words.

He muzzled Gould in the hallway leading to the press room. "Come on," he said, "let's get out of here. I've been here six weeks now. The place is getting on my nerves."

"Okay, Jim," said Gould. "We go after tomorrow's workout."

It was a vicious Braddock who went to work on his mates on Sunday afternoon. Although the newspaper delegation remained status quo, an entire army of Jim's admirers from Hudson County, led by Judge Robert V. Kinkead, flooded the camp to watch what was destined to be his last drill at camp.

He boxed only three rounds in all, one with Pross and two with Big Jack McCarthy. He nearly tore Pross' jaw off with a right hand in the first heat and then belabored McCarthy fiercely and vigorously in the next two. His offense was a delight to the crowd—but the more important details perhaps went unnoticed. His condition was absolutely superb and his defense against McCarthy's rights well-nigh perfect. McCarthy was able to land but two right hands in two rounds and both were light blows—blows that barely touched Jim's jaw.

His surly mood vanished with that last drill. He was happy now—camp was to break. As Doc Robb put him on the scales, he asked the author how he had "looked."

"Wonderful," came the reply. "On the form you showed today, you just can't lose."

He weighed just 196 pounds as camp broke.

CHAPTER NINETEEN

AWAITING THE BIG DAY

BAER...

THOSE last few days before the fight, spent in New York, were sweltering ones. The city was in the midst of a broiling heat wave. But fortunately, Braddock's reactions this time were not similar to the reactions he had experienced when he left Saratoga and came to New York for the Loughran fight in 1929.

Braddock worked Monday afternoon at Stillman's gymnasium. He weighed 194 pounds following the drill before a packed house—and Gould and Robb were so delighted with his condition that they decided there would be no more boxing until the gong called him to the middle of the ring.

Short road runs on Tuesday and Wednesday mornings completed the training siege.

While Braddock took things easy those two days, Gould was furiously busy. On Tuesday, he and Ancil Hoffman appeared before the New York Commission at the Commission's regular meeting to discuss the referee question which had been popping all over the sports pages.

Gould objected to Jack Dempsey, not on any personal grounds (though some months later he was to become embroiled with the former champion over a "White Hope" tournament which he took as an affront to Braddock) but because Dempsey had in the past owned a "piece" of Baer.

"Anybody the commission names but Dempsey is okay with us," he said.

Hoffman, on the other hand, objected very strenuously to Arthur Donovan, who the year before had refereed the Carnera-Baer fight. Hoffman's objections were based on the fact that Donovan's score card after that fight did not quite coincide with the manner in which Hoffman and Baer thought the fight had gone. "At the end of the tenth round," complained Hoffman with the air of a man who had been done a great wrong, "he (Donovan) had five rounds for Carnera and five rounds for us. We won every round."

In what he no doubt considered a laudable attempt to see justice done Baer, Hoffman turned over to the commission, the names of five officials who would be agreeable to the champion. They were George Blake, Gene Tunney, Lt. Jack Kennedy, Ed Dickerson, and Lt. Commander Jess Kenworthy. Several of these gentlemen were in distant seas at the time. And not one had a referee's license in New York State.

Chairman Phelan disposed of Hoffman's list brusquely. "The man who referees the fight will be a licensed New York official," he said. "We are not going out of town for referees. Our men are capable enough."

"Okay," retorted Hoffman, "but I am telling you now that Baer will walk right out of the ring if Donovan is named."

The discussion then turned to the matter of forfeits.

"Er—ahem," said Phelan, turning first to Gould, "you have not as yet posted your forfeit to guarantee Braddock's appearance."

"I am sorry, General," responded Gould glibly, "but we haven't got the money. But if you don't think Braddock will show up for the fight, I'll bring him down here and leave him on deposit!"

Phelan fussed a bit, but Gould put up no forfeit—neither did he fetch Braddock as a "deposit."

Nor did Baer put up a forfeit, either. Hoffman wasn't going to take any chances on losing $2,500—just in case Baer did walk out of the ring.

The day before the fight saw Braddock and Gould make a flying trip across the river, to pay a visit to judge Kinkead in his chambers in Jersey City. The Judge immediately halted court and staged a mock trial during which, believe it or not, Braddock, the defendant, was sentenced "to win the world's heavyweight championship."

Braddock then paid a short visit to his family in North Bergen, after which Gould drove him back to New York for a sound sleep the night before the fight.

New York buzzed with fight talk on the eve of the championship bout. Baer ruled more of a favorite than ever. Odds of eight to one and ten to one and twelve to one on the champion were quoted freely.

But the overwhelming odds in the champion's favor merely made Joe Gould more cocky.

"The more lightly he takes Braddock, the better it is going to be for us," he declared.

Baer was taking Braddock lightly.

The champion simply felt that Braddock was not in his class. He had loafed and clowned continually at camp, in the belief that all he needed to lick Braddock was "a shave and a shampoo," a training routine employed successfully on certain occasions by John L. Sullivan many years before. Baer's Asbury Park workouts had been desultory. They had lacked the prolonged ferocity of Braddock's sessions at Loch Sheldrake. The champion would fight for seconds and then loaf and clown for minutes. Dynamite Jackson, one sparmate, had clubbed him regularly in his drills. But through it all, the bronzed Baer had laughed and grinned and kidded—absolutely certain it was all one big joke—on Braddock and the New York Commission.

Yet with all of Baer's miserable showing in camp, the newspapermen (recalling how Baer had fooled everybody, even eagle-eyed Bill Brown the year before when he had looked so pitiful while training for Primo Carnera) could not possibly have done otherwise but install Baer as the favorite.

The records, for one thing, pointed to an overwhelming Baer triumph.

Over a period of ten years, Braddock had lost over twenty fights. Against these two score defeats—Baer had been beaten only seven times in his career—and HAD NOT SUFFERED DEFEAT FOR FOUR YEARS! Away back in 1931, when he was still a raw novice of 22, Paulino Uzcudun had eked out a very close decision over him in a bristling fight at Reno, Nevada. From then on, Baer had scored one spectacular victory over another, and his last two victories had come at the expense of Max Schmeling and Primo Carnera, by means of knockouts.

Not only that, but he was the younger man of the two—and he was by far the bigger, as well. He figured to enter the ring with a weight advantage of almost 20 pounds over Braddock—certainly nothing to be sneezed at in a fifteen-round fight. And Baer knew it. "I'm just too big for Braddock," he would confide to the writers.

No wonder then that the overwhelming majority of newspapermen were for Baer.

One critic wrote that Baer outclassed "Braddock even more than Tunney outclassed Heeney," and declared that Braddock, when a sparring mate for Heeney at Fairhaven, in July, 1928, "was about the only one of Heeney's crew that Heeney could lick in a rehearsal match."

That the Braddock of 1928, only two years out of the amateurs, wasn't even a light-heavyweight (he weighed around 170 pounds at the time) and that he went into those workouts with Heeney at a weight disadvantage of around 35 pounds (Heeney scaled 203½ for the Tunney fight) apparently was overlooked.

Other writers declared openly "only a miracle can win for Braddock." A magazine article concerning the fight was captioned "Midsummer Night's Massacre," lending to the affair the ghastly color of a Shakespearean tragedy. Most of the headlines picked "Baer by a Knockout." A few of the more daring declared it would be Baer "in five rounds." Others, almost apologetically, it seemed, said it might go "seven rounds." In the midst of this, articles by Damon Runyon, of the New York *American*, and Wilbur Wood, sports editor of the New York Sun, declaring that odds of eight to one were silly whenever two "well-conditioned heavyweights met and that expert opinion very often was wrong when it pointed overwhelmingly one way (citing the Tunney-Dempsey fight as an instance) fell upon deaf ears.

Yes, Braddock had few supporters indeed. Only Murray Robinson, of the Newark *Star Eagle,* Ed Van Every, of the *Sun,* Edward J. Neil, of the *Associated Press,* Jackie Farrell, radio broadcaster, the author, and one or two others; at the most, hazarded the opinion that Braddock might surprise the world and beat Baer.

Despite the terrific one-sidedness of newspaper opinion and its reflection in the betting odds, Braddock received a considerable and surprising amount of support from within the cauliflower ranks. Baer, of course, ruled the favorite here, too. But not by any overwhelming numbers.

Like the few newspapermen who had Braddock leanings, those members of the fistic gentry who inclined to the Jerseyite did so because of his remarkable condition.

One of the shrewdest fight managers in the business, Joe Jacobs, wrote a series of articles in the New York *Evening Post* and throughout every one of his earlier pieces, pointed out that Braddock was in magnificent condition and that Baer was not. In his last article, however, Jacobs switched and picked Baer. He admitted afterwards that he had permitted a Coast newspaperman to sway his own judgement. Gene Tunney, a Braddock man as far back as 1928, also changed around and picked Baer. Jack Dempsey, Primo Carnera, Mike Jacobs, Billy Roche, Nate Lewis, Mickey Walker, and Joe Louis, a young colored fighter who was booming along rapidly himself at the time, liked Baer, too.

But Braddock supporters were by no means scarce. Tommy Loughran, who had licked both Baer and Braddock, picked Braddock. So did Jess Willard and Tony Canzoneri and Georgie Ward and Billy McCarney and Bob Olin and Jimmy McLarnin and Jack Sharkey and Billy Gibson and Charley Harvey and Jack Johnson and Benny Leonard.

Notwithstanding, when the day of the fight dawned, Braddock entered the ring possessed in the public mind of only the proverbial "Chinaman's chance."

CHAPTER TWENTY

JUNE 13TH, 1935, A.D.

IT WAS feverishly warm in New York on the day of the fight. The thermometer soared past the 80-degree mark at noon and kept climbing. Thousands of fight fans crowded around the entrance to the State Building in downtown New York during lunch hour, to await the appearance of the champion and challenger for the weighing-in.

The challenger, accompanied by Joe Gould, Solly Seeman, Doc Robb, and also Mike Cantwell, Baer's former trainer who had now declared himself a member of the Braddock forces, arrived first and fought his way through the crowd to the basement of the State Building where the weighing-in was to take place.

Baer was half an hour late. Finally, he, too, elbowed his way through the mob. As he entered the dressing room, he spied Braddock seated on a chair. He made for Jimmy right away, hand extended, a half-smile, a half-sneer on his face.

Before he could get to Braddock, however, Gould, dressed in a pair of sea-green trousers and a yellow polo shirt, jumped at him.

"Get away from here," he shouted at the champion. "Get away from here, you bum. If you've got anything to say—say it tonight—in the ring."

Baer made another attempt to speak but Gould jeered at him again, and at the top of his voice.

"Oh, all right," said Baer peevishly, "I only wanted to say hello," and he moved away.

"I know what he wanted to say," roared Gould. "He wanted to tell Braddock that Braddock was lucky to be fighting him for the championship and that his brother, Buddy, could knock Braddock out. I was tipped off. Well, I fixed his wagon."

At this moment, Baer became involved in another altercation.

A rather heavily set person, wearing a straw hat and a blue suit, had stopped the titleholder. The restrainer was Mike Cantwell, who the year before had trained Baer for the fight in which Max had ascended to the championship. Harsh language began to fly about.

General Phelan finally stepped in between them.

"Here, here," the New York commission head admonished, "cut that out! I'm running this thing and I want order and quiet!"

Cantwell shut up. The fighters then shed their clothes and stepped upon the scales. Braddock weighed 191¾, almost ten pounds more than he had weighed for Lasky but a few months before. Baer weighed 209½ —a difference of about 18 pounds in his favor. Braddock's skin was white; Baer's was a copper color. Braddock was bigger in the legs. Baer was bigger in the shoulders. "That's where he gets his punching power from," someone remarked.

The photographers asked them to square off and pose for pictures. They did. The first flash bulb to go off, however, caused Baer to jump.

"Better be careful of those things," he grumbled to the cameramen. But they paid no attention to him and went merrily on with their business. They must have taken at least two hundred pictures. Through it all, Baer seemed more nervous than Braddock. But Jimmy was not entirely calm. It was a moment to test any one's nerves. He winked at his friends, but the winks seemed just a bit forced. Later, Dr. William Walker's report revealed that Braddock was the more nervous of the two.

"Baer's pulse was 68 normal and 83 after exercise," reported Dr. Walker. "It went back to normal in 45 seconds. Braddock's pulse was 88 normal and 99 after exercise, but required only 35 seconds to go back to normal. Braddock seemed a bit tightened up. His blood pressure was 140 over 90 while Baer's was 150 over 100."

While the pictures were being taken, Gould, standing close to Baer, ready for anything that might be required in the way of verbal cannonading, noted that the champion was gazing intently into Braddock's eyes.

"Take a good look at him," sneered Gould, "so you'll recognize him tonight."

Baer said nothing.

"Take another good look at him," Gould continued, trying to nettle Baer. Baer again refused to reply.

"I had better get away from here," Gould finally snickered, "before I start a fight."

The photographers eventually finished; the fighters dressed and repaired from the basement dressing room to the commission's offices on the fifth floor of the State Building. There, behind closed doors, a long conference took place. Hoffman had brought along a specially designed boxing glove, used in California and Illinois, which he wanted the New York solons to sanction for the title fight.

"Nothing doing," snorted Gould, looking at the gloves. "These mitts are made to protect Baer's hands."

A violent discussion ensued. It ended in the usual manner, the commission announcing that no changes could be considered and that the regulation New York gloves would be used. Hoffman, peeved no end, made it plain that he felt he was "being kicked around." "I can't get a favor around here," he protested, "and I've got the champion."

Eventually, Baer and his manager left the conference in something of a dudgeon. Hoffman walked sullenly through the cordon of newspapermen but Baer, spotting Mike Cantwell in the crowd, stopped long enough to take a verbal shot at his old trainer. Cantwell, however, refused to notice him.

A moment later, when Braddock and Gould emerged from the conference room, Cantwell grabbed Braddock by the arm.

"You'll lick him sure," he said to the challenger. "I can tell he's worried stiff by just looking at him. I know him. He's worried."

Braddock smiled, and after answering a few questions fired at him by the newspapermen, left for his hotel, the Mayflower, on Central Park West. Solly Seeman and Doc Robb accompanied him.

It was late in the afternoon, when Gould, who had rushed to the Garden to attend to ticket matters, rejoined his fighter at the Mayflower. By this time, Braddock had finished his nap.

A long conference followed between fighter, manager and seconds. As Braddock lay sprawled on the bed, Gould, Robb and Seeman, seated around him, discussed the battle plans for the last time. Braddock was to jab quickly and then at once, either step in close or circle away from Baer's right hand.

"In and out," directed Gould. "Never stand still like Carnera did and let him get a pot shot at you. You don't have to worry about his left. just jab and hook with your left, and watch his right. After the first three or four rounds, he'll be finished. When he finds out the kind of condition you're in and that you aren't afraid of him, he'll quit."

Not very long afterwards, they were rushing by automobile to Madison Square Garden's huge bowl on the flats at Astoria, Long Island. Once there, Braddock laid himself down on a couch in the dressing room assigned to the challenger. Doc Robb threw a blanket over him. Friends began to drop in to wish him luck, but Robb instructed Jimmy to lay off shaking hands. Gould, perhaps more nervous than his fighter, first walked around the Bowl twice with Sam Cohen, a boyhood pal, and then returned to the dressing room to wait. Commissioners and deputies began to appear. The tape and the foul-proof cup were examined. Through it all Gould kept up a rapid fire of conversation. He was excited. Braddock on the other hand was remarkably calm.

Then, just a little before ten o'clock, came the call for the march to the ring.

CHAPTER TWENTY-ONE

VICTORY—AND A NEW CHAMPION

BAER
CLOWNED

A DEAFENING ovation thundered across the Bowl as Braddock, clad in a blue silk bathrobe, clambered through the ropes first. Baer entered a few minutes later. The champion seemed a bit worried underneath to those who knew him closely. But he nodded and smiled with a forced ease to all those he recognized at the ringside.

The entrance of Johnny McAvoy of Brooklyn into the ring to act as third man surprised both corners. All hands had expected Arthur Donovan to get the nomination. Charlie Lynch and George Kelly were announced as the judges. It looked like a great night for the Irish.

Challenger and champion then were formally introduced to the crowd, after which McAvoy called them to the center of the ring for final instructions.

Hearts began thump-thump-thumping away as the men went back to their corners, shed their bathrobes, and awaited the bell.

Finally, after what seemed like an interminable wait, the gong sounded.

Before the vast crowd of 40,000 realized what had happened, Braddock had done to Baer what the champion himself had done in the first round to Max Schmeling in 1933. The challenger had caught Baer completely by surprise with an aggressive, well-directed attack that disturbed Max both psychologically and physically.

The Jerseyite rushed in close to the champion. Baer met him with a stiff left, but Jimmy took the punch and buried a hook into Baer's side. It spun Baer around a bit. The champion was open for a right and Braddock grabbed his golden opportunity. He cracked Baer with a stinging smash to the jaw. The crowd yelled. Baer sneered. Braddock let him have another right. Then a left. Then, to the savage delight of the crowd, and to Baer's great discomfiture, the not at all awe-struck challenger bounced another terrific right off the champion's jaw.

Those three early rights, all of them robust smashes, stung Baer to the quick, but the champion haughtily sneered and clowned his way through the round. just before the session ended, Braddock climaxed things by spraying him with left hands. The titleholder had lost the round by a mile, but he walked to his corner with such an air of grandeur and superiority that the crowd still felt he could end the fight any moment he cared to.

Jimmy started a wild right hand swing as the second round began. Baer smirked. They traded lefts. Baer sneered. But as he did, Braddock thrust a loud jab in his face. Again Baer sneered. Again Braddock jabbed him. The crowd chortled with glee and Braddock spread his left royally across the titleholder's pan. Baer started a ferocious rush at Jimmy—his first of the fight—but it fizzled out. Braddock nailed him with an uppercut. The blow snapped the champion's head back with a jar. He grimaced, went into a crouch, and roared at Braddock. Braddock retorted by pushing a left in his face. Whereupon Baer pulled up his tights and took a deep breath. He smiled—but it was a puzzling smile. As the round ended, he gave Braddock a patronizing pat on the back. Braddock, however, apparently was unappreciative of this little nicety on the champion's part: he walked to his corner without saying "thanks."

Braddock lashed for the head as the third began—Baer for the body. Braddock landed the more frequently. Some of Baer's stomach smashes were close to the danger line and Joe Gould yelled madly from the corner for Baer to keep his punches up. Braddock stung the champ with two lefts and then a hard right to the jaw. Two more such rights caused Fancy Max to clown. The champion now drove for the body. The punch was visibly low. Braddock motioned for Baer "to keep 'em up." And then right—crossed him viciously. It was a lusty hit. The crowd began to wonder whether Max really was "letting the thing go for a while for the movies."

Braddock held Baer even in the fourth round. The champion, unable to reach Braddock's head because the Jerseyite was steadily circling away from his right, began playing for the ribs. He got in some heavy smashes to Jimmy's left side and a red splotch soon appeared there. Braddock drove a volley of lefts to the head. They got into a clinch and Baer tried to wrestle Braddock around. For this breach of ring etiquette he drew the wrath of the referee. The crowd booed, too. Gould's voice also was heard, protesting violently that Baer was fighting "dirty." Baer raised his hand to the crowd, as if to apologize. He then thundered a right to the ribs, but Braddock pumped back with a left, followed by a right. Baer scored with a hard right-hand smash to the jaw. The blow failed, however, to disturb Jimmy. Baer also got in a savage uppercut, only to receive two hard rights in return just before the bell sounded.

The fifth saw Braddock score with a series of annoying lefts and thereafter to circle steadily to Baer's left—to the champ's open discomfiture. Baer was palpably annoyed as he realized that Braddock was continually outside the range of his pet blow. His annoyance was reflected in a backhand punch and he was warned by the referee to abstain. He did catch Braddock with a stinging uppercut. But Braddock retaliated with a stream of long jabs and then hooked when in close. The challenger either darted inside the champ's right—or quickly moved out of range—always in the same direction (to his own and away from Baer's right). Baer tried to box Braddock but floundered all over the ring, finally giving it up as a bad job. Braddock showered him with lefts and rights. Baer again was guilty of a backhand punch—and was penalized the round. But Braddock had won the session on points anyway.

Baer drove three terrific uppercuts home with the start of the sixth session to draw blood from Jim's mouth and nose. In this moment of distress, the Jerseyite's left hand proved a tremendous defensive weapon. It almost boomed as it stopped Baer's rushes. They staged a mad slugfest at close quarters. Braddock astounded the crowd by hammering the champ vigorously around the body. Baer became enraged and fired such a damaging body barrage right back that he forced Jim to gasp for wind. Quick to take advantage, Baer leaped in and hurled a terrific series of punches at Braddock. But he was too anxious and too wild. Braddock's left dug into his face and the champion's left eye seemed to be closing. It was the champion's round, according to the consensus.

In the seventh round, Baer staged a slashing outburst. He tore into Jimmy with a series of vicious uppercuts. They were followed by two fearful rights to the jaw and as Braddock tried desperately to stay him with lefts, Baer just stormed in and powdered the body. During this mixup, he landed one of the hardest punches of the fight, a crashing right to the ribs that shook Braddock from head to foot. The champion now butchered Braddock in close, then slipped back and smartly cracked him on the jaw with a right. But Braddock absorbed all those punches without toppling. Baer was puzzled and serious as he went to his corner.

The crowd, impressed by the titleholder's showing in the seventh, expectantly waited for something to happen in the eighth. But it was Braddock who scored first—with a savage right to the temple. An instant later, he had bounced a slam-bang right off Baer's jaw—and as the crowd let out a wild yell, Baer, apparently badly hurt, wobbled, and started to sag to the canvas.

But just as the crowd leaped to its feet, Baer sneered, showed his teeth, and, roaring, rushed at Braddock. He had not been hurt; he had merely been faking. Braddock, however, apparently warned against such an occurrence, was ready for him. He met Baer's rush with a solid left and then threw two rights at the titleholder. The left exploded squarely in Baer's face. The rights which might have done real damage both missed their mark.

Braddock battled tenaciously in the ninth, punching, punching, punching without a let up. Baer fought in his usual spurts, but early in the round was guilty of a low punch and late in the round was guilty of a backhand. They were costly infractions. He bullied and mauled Braddock considerably in this session. His uppercuts drew blood freely from the challenger's nose. Though his best punches had failed to knock the well-conditioned challenger off his feet, they had certainly given Baer the edge in this session. But his violations had cost him the round, Referee McAvoy announced to the judges.

The tenth was Baer's by a commanding margin. He ripped away at Braddock with an uppercut again, punched him with rights and taunted him with words—but through it all, did no serious damage. As a matter of fact, though Baer won the round, Braddock, always circling away from danger according to the pre-battle plan, got in two vital punches before the session ended. One was a hard right to the head and the other was a similar punch to the mouth. Baer spat blood as he went to his corner— and his expression was not one of a confident titleholder. The fight had now gone ten rounds—and taken plenty out of him.

He began to realize now that the fight probably would go the limit and that as things stood, Braddock had the edge in points because of the earlier rounds. He realized that illegal punches had cost him a couple of sessions. He also realized that he was tiring.

He went out for the eleventh knowing that he had to do or die and the round was only a few seconds old when the Bowl trembled with the wildest excitement. Baer had landed his Sunday punch, his looping overhand right, the same punch which had knocked out Schmeling in 1933, and a year later sent Carnera to the boards a dozen times. Braddock, however, not only took Baer's best punch without going down—to the champion's sheer dismay—but actually retaliated with a flood of lefts. Condition was beginning to tell now. Baer was unable to get his face away from those lefts. Desperately, Baer charged in again, grimly determined to bash Braddock down at all costs. But it was not to be. Braddock wobbled and swayed before Baer's rushes—but stayed on his feet. He lost the round—but won the fight. Baer knew he had shot his bolt when the round ended.

The twelfth was a humdinger. Early in this round, Braddock landed his best punch—a devastating right hand. Baer stalled awhile—then lurched punches wildly into the night air. Braddock, stepping about, cracked him with sharp lefts and rights. Baer finally found the ribs, but Braddock hooked to the chin and split a right to the jaw. Then, Braddock began to run riot with his left. No matter which way Baer turned, Braddock's left messed him. Aggravated no end, Baer forgot all the rules and hit on the break. There was a roar from Braddock's corner. Gould was shrieking madly above the tumult of the crowd. Baer turned to answer Gould. As he did, Braddock pasted him with a right to the chin. The champion was more furious than ever now. So furious that he unfortunately and no doubt unintentionally rammed a smashing right to Braddock's ear right after the bell. It was a terrific punch—and it gave Braddock his only souvenir of the fight—a bad ear.

Gould was almost violent as Baer landed that post-bell punch. He hopped into the ring like a madman, started a rush towards the champion's corner, and shrieked:

"Why don't you fight clean, you —— ———— ————?"

"I am fightin' clean," Baer hissed through swollen lips.

Before Gould could say another word, the cops had manhandled him back to the corner. For an instant it seemed as though he would not only be thrown out of the ring, but rushed out of the arena as well. Somehow or other, however, he managed to stay.

By this time, Jimmy Johnston, clad in a gray-checked coat, light blue trousers, deep blue shirt, yellow tie, and a straw hat, had appeared in Braddock's corner, too. Sensing that a Braddock victory was imminent and that the hated Baer was to be shorn of his title, Johnston's joy knew no bounds. His voice began to be heard with Gould's over the exhortations of the crowd.

"Keep yer left up," Johnston yelled.

"Make him fight clean," thundered Gould.

"Just be careful, Jimmy," implored the crowd.

Baer, it seemed, had not a friend.

As the tiring champion grew weaker and weaker, Braddock grew stronger. The challenger realized his legs were in splendid shape. He was deeply grateful now for the roadwork he had done at Sheldrake. Well-conditioned legs moved him gracefully about, and the arms which had been so well conditioned on the wharves did the rest. He stepped around Baer easily and prodded him vigorously as he did. He just rained jabs and hooks on the champion in the thirteenth round. They were not terrific punches. But they stung as they poured in on Baer like so much hail.

Braddock rolled up a tremendous edge in this session. It clinched the fight for him.

Baer's only hope after the thirteenth was a knockout. Desperately, he tried to score one. But Braddock stifled him at every turn. Baer knew when the gong ended the fifteenth and final round that the title had changed hands. He put his arms around Jimmy and embraced him. Impatiently, the crowd waited for Al Frazin's announcement. And when Frazin (who was subbing for the ailing Joe Humphreys) finally barked into the microphone—"Winner—and NEW CHAMPION"—a roar that was like Niagara itself reverberated across Astoria's flats.

Yes, James J. Braddock, of North Bergen, the man who "couldn't win"—had performed the miracle.

The man who "didn't have a chance"—the man for whom Ancil Hoffman had requested an ambulance—the man for whom Baer was too big—the man who had been dubbed the weakest challenger in the history of the heavyweight championship—the man who was slow and couldn't move around—the man who had lost some twenty fights in his career—the man who had not even been rated among the heavyweights for 1935 and who had been listed but TENTH AND LAST among the light-heavyweights—the man who was too old to fight young Baer—the man who was married and the father of three children—the man who had been on relief and subsisted only on hash for a year—the man who had walked around the streets just a few months before with holes in his shoes—the man who had done his roadwork looking for work on the docks—the man whose hand was broken and who thought his career was ended in September, 1933—the man who had been thrown successively against Corn Griffin, John Henry Lewis and Art Lasky in the expectations that he would prove a splendid "stooge" for them—this man had confounded everybody, he had confounded the champion, he had confounded the newspapermen and he had confounded the general public as well by winning the world's heavyweight championship!

CHAPTER TWENTY-TWO

THE END OF A PERFECT NIGHT

CHAMPION !!!

BRADDOCK had almost as tough a fight to get to his dressing room after the fight as he had had in the ring with Baer. Finally, the policemen delivered Jimmy intact to one of the low-ceilinged buildings on the edge of the Bowl. There, as a never-ending mob milled in and out, the new champion held court.

"It was great to win," he almost whispered through a microphone, held together by an excited announcer for a national network. "I wanted to do so for the wife and kiddies. For six months, I have been promising them that I would bring home the world's heavyweight title and I'm glad I can go home tonight and make good my promise. Sure I'm happy. Who wouldn't be?"

Just then, Gould burst into the room, almost delirious with joy. He jabbered incoherently, grabbed Braddock, kissed him and then kissed and hugged Trainer Doc Robb and seconds Whitey Bimstein and Ray Arcel, who had been in Braddock's corner. Newspapermen poured into the room.

"Baer claims he broke his hands in the fifth," one scribe remarked.

191

"Yeh!" shouted Gould with the air of a man who has just been left a million dollars. "That's TOO bad. Honest, I'm sorry for him."

As the reporters fired an incessant barrage of questions at Braddock, Robb bundled the new champion up. Policemen made a flying wedge. And Braddock, as he rushed to a cab outside, failed to notice his mother and father who had fought their way to the dressing room door—only to be halted there.

The celebration that followed at the Mayflower Hotel lasted until daybreak. Hundreds upon hundreds of persons filtered into the modest suite on the 16th floor to congratulate the new champion. Through it all, Gould kept yelling at the top of his voice. Albertanti kept cheering for Corn Griffin. Newspapermen kept asking excited questions and getting excited answers in return. If the fight was fought over once, it was fought over a dozen times. There weren't many "I-told-you" boys around—but those that were made up in volume what they lacked in numbers.

Braddock, his most cherished ambition realized, sat on a bed, clad in a pair of blue pajamas, looking weary, but happy. His face was a bit puffed and one of his eyes a bit closed. And there was a bit of adhesive tape on the left ear—the ear which had caught Baer's after-the-bell right-hand punch as the 12th round had ended. They were his lone "souvenirs" of the fight.

The photographers kept him busy indeed. He must have posed for close to 300 pictures. Flashbulbs blinded him for over an hour. An *Associated Press* photographer made a paper crown and placed it upon his head. It made a swell picture. Every camera in the place clicked for that one.

The photographers had run out of flashbulbs when there was a roar from the outside room. The champion's wife, Mae, who had listened to the broadcast of the fight at the home of her parents in Guttenberg, N. J., had rushed across the Hudson River to meet her husband. The crowd instantly made way for her. She literally flew into Jimmy's arms. Hugs. Kisses. The picture hungry photographers rushed downstairs to their automobiles and returned soon—this time with cases of flashbulbs. They again went to work with a zest that was delightful to the onlookers, but a bit taxing now to the tired new champion.

Finally, Jimmy pleaded with the photographers to leave him alone. Eventually they got out. One of the rooms was cleared, and only a few close friends from Hudson County remained therein with Jimmy and Mae.

In the reception room, however, the din continued unabated. Joe Jacobs walked in. He took a ribbing for having switched from Braddock at the last moment. Judge Kinkead appeared, to the great delight of Albertanti, who started to "rib" the judge. Eddie Neil, of the *Associated Press*, who had collected $250 on a 25 to 1 bet on Braddock, marched in with a wide smile and congratulations. Murray Lewin, of the *Daily Mirror*, was with him.

In the midst of it all, Albertanti kept repeating over and over again:

"Hooray for Corn Griffin."

Telegrams piled in by the hundreds. They came from New York, from Hudson County, from Chicago, from the Pacific Coast, and even from an individual in distant Saskatchewan.

"Jingo," jabbered Gould, wiping the sweat from his brow, "here's a cable from London—yes, it's from London."

"Who sent it?" asked Albertanti.

"John Mortimer," perspired Gould. "He says 'Remember Tom Heeney?' " (Mortimer had been one of Heeney's managers when Braddock had served as a sparring partner for the Anzac at Fairhaven in 1928.)

Albertanti, opening telegrams himself, shouted:

"Here's one from Cornelius Vanderbilt."

"What is he—a middleweight or a heavyweight?" asked Gould.

The messenger boys came in with another bundle of yellow and blue envelopes.

"Whoopee," ejaculated Gould. "Here's a telegram from Tunney sending congratulations. You had better send him an answer right away. Thank him, but tell him he should have stuck to the ship."

The room was jammed with well-wishers and it was sweltering hot— but no one made a move to go home, even though it was past four o'clock by this time. Braddock had long since been spirited away to another part of the hotel for rest.

Gould and Albertanti kept merrily on, the latter pouring out the drinks for a steady stream of new arrivals while the former, talking to himself half of the time, kept reading the telegrams.

"Listen to this," he suddenly chortled, "here's a telegram from two Irishmen in the state of Washington. It's signed 'Mulligan and Sullivan.' "

"And here's another from all those Irish movie actors who sent us those telegrams before the fight," he broke out an instant later.

The actors who had telegraphed their congratulations were Pat O'Brien, Frank McHugh, Jimmy Cagney and Allen Jenkins. Early the afternoon of the fight, while Braddock was sleeping at the hotel, they had started wiring from the Coast. By the time Braddock entered the ring, he had received no less than four sets of telegrams from them. Their final and congratulatory wires read, "We knew you'd do it, kid."

Still the telegrams continued to pour in. "I felt that left hook in the 12th round way out here in Boston," insisted Jay Barry from the Hub . . . "We want you to know how happy we are over your victory," declared Mr. and Mrs. Lou Gehrig . . . The Ancient Order of Hibernians from Meriden, Conn., sent sincere congratulations . . . the mother of the late Ernie Schaaf also felicitated the new champion.

"Wheeeeeee—eeeeeee!" roared Albertanti suddenly. "What do you think? Here's a telegram from Columbus, Georgia, from Corn Griffin!"

Sure enough it was.

"Congratulations to the new champion from the Cracker who started him on the way up. Would like to meet you again," the missive read.

"Hooray for Corn Griffin," shouted Albertanti at the top of his voice.

"Hooray for Corn Griffin," shouted everybody in unison. "Hooray, Hooray, Hooray."

By this time—daybreak had arrived. The first rays of dawn had glided across Central Park and were streaming softly into the room. Gould slowly spread himself upon a bed.

"Well," he mumbled, "I'm going to sleep right here with all these telegrams."

"I am, too," said Albertanti.

While they slept, the telegrams continued unabated . . . congratulations from Johnny Evers and Alabama Pitts . . . from Les Patrick, far off in Victoria, British Columbia . . . from Pete Latzo, whose jaw Braddock had broken . . . from Billy Petrolle . . . from Joe Monte . . . from Johnny Wilson . . . from Leo Lomski . . . from Pop Canzoneri and the boys at Marlboro . . . from Harry Ebbetts . . . from William Brady, who in his day had managed Jim Corbett and Jim Jeffries . . . from Art Lasky . . . from Kelly Petillo, who had just won the 500-mile auto race at Indianapolis . . . and so on . . . and so on . . . ad infinitum.

Yes, Braddock's was a popular victory.

CHAPTER TWENTY-THREE

CHAMPION A YEAR

JAMES J. BRADDOCK had been world's heavyweight champion for a little over thirteen months when the final chapter of this book was written. In those thirteen months there occurred in the heavyweight division a kaleidoscopic series of events which for a protracted period made Braddock the Forgotten King.

When the hysteria which followed the dethronement of Max Baer by the Jerseyite finally ended and speculation began as to the new champion's most probable foe in his first title defense—there loomed above all others as likely foes for Braddock—Max Baer, Max Schmeling and Primo Carnera—all ex-champions—and young Joe Louis, the Detroit Negro.

There were many who felt that Braddock owed Baer, the man from whom he had won the title, a return fight and Gould and Braddock, who felt likewise, openly declared the Californian could have a return crack any time he asked for it.

Some persons, of course, put the ugly interpretation on the willingness of the new champion to give Baer a return shot.

"This is all part of a pre-arranged plan," they said. "Baer wants to go over to Germany and pick up some big dough for fighting Schmeling, but he doesn't want to take a chance on being jobbed out of his title over there. So, he is letting Braddock mind the title until he comes back."

Others had plausible stories, too. But they coursed along a different tack.

"Baer is getting ready for this young Louis fellow," they explained. "If Louis ever beats Carnera, he'll mean a tremendous gate and Baer wants to be ready. But he knows the government will never stand for a mixed match for the heavyweight championship after what happened when Johnson fought Jeffries so he's letting Braddock mind the title until after he fights Louis. And after he polishes Louis off all he will have to do to get his title back will be to call Braddock on the phone. Yes, sir. You just mark my words."

How utterly absurd these very positive assertions were—time itself was soon to tell.

Newspapers were in the very midst of their life stories of James J. Braddock, the new heavyweight champion, when the greatest ascension in the history of boxing began. On the night of June 25th, 1935, only twelve days after Braddock had beaten Baer, a smooth-moving Negro out of Detroit named Joseph Barrow Louis stepped into the ring at the Yankee Stadium and electrified the fistic world by hurling the vast Primo Carnera to a technical knockout in six sizzling rounds, scoring his kayo after a most brilliant exhibition of punching.

On August 7th, at Chicago, Louis, still considered in some quarters as a bit immature, flattened Kingfish Levinsky in just one round, and just about six weeks later (on September 24th) he moved back to the Yankee Stadium and this time, "before a goggle-eyed house of over 80,000 persons, he whistled Baer right out of the premises in just four rounds, the spectators looking on with utter amazement as Baer was counted out while in the full possession of his senses and while resting on one hand and one knee!

Nor was that all.

As if the Carnera, Levinsky and Baer knockouts weren't enough to propel him squarely into the public eye as THE man Braddock would have to fight to keep his title, the Black Menace now proceeded to give an even more devastating exhibition of his punching power. He met Paulino Uzcudun at Madison Square Garden on the 13th of December, and poor Paulino, who never before had been knocked out, was felled after a brave fight by the first serious punch that Louis fired at him, the clash ending in the fourth round. And a few weeks later, he hurtled back to Chicago and there on January 17th, 1936, flattened Charlie Retzlaff, of Duluth, in less than two minutes of fighting.

By this time, of course, Joe Louis had become the sensation of sensations. His amazing series of knockouts over ex-champions and ordinary foes alike, had projected him so high in the pugilistic constellation, that he no longer was "the logical challenger"—he was "the uncrowned champion!" He actually was listed in the annual boxing rankings as the Number One Heavyweight of the world, while Braddock, the champion, was ranked Number Two.

The rush of newspaper publicity attendant to Louis' glittering knockouts was absolutely stupendous. Headlines, streamers, cartoons, columns, photographs, feature articles and editorials literally roared forth in never-ending torrents about this pugilistic phenom of all time. "Here at last," everybody cried, "is the perfect fighter." Within a few months the name of Joe Louis had all but become a legend—and a terrifying one—to the heavyweight division. Still a youth of 21, they began saying of him already that "there would be no more worlds for him to conquer after he got through with Braddock." No wonder then that the colored race began to look eagerly and expectantly towards that day when this clean-cut young lad who had first seen the light of day on May 13th, 1914, at Lexington, Alabama, would ascend the heavyweight throne.

In the face of this never-ending tumult for Louis, which greeted them wherever they went and which shuffled them rudely and unceremoniously into the background, James J. Braddock and Joe Gould conducted themselves magnificently. It was grating on the nerves to win a world's heavyweight championship only to find out somebody else was being hailed as "the uncrowned champion." It was galling to discover, when booking exhibition tours, that the Man of the Hour was not Braddock, but Joseph Barrow Louis. It was not at all pleasant to realize that this Louis person was costing Braddock thousands of dollars that would have just rolled his way—had Louis not come along to dominate the picture in such spectacular fashion. But there was absolutely nothing Braddock could do but sit back and bide his time.

Talk of Louis was inevitable wherever the champion went. On one occasion, the author asked Jimmy:

"How would you fight him?"

"The same as I fought Griffiths," Braddock replied slowly. "I'd make him come to me. He can be hit."

"We don't even consider any other challengers," Gould told newspapermen during interviews. "We want Louis. He is the outstanding challenger."

There never, was any resentment or ill-feeling towards the Negro. Braddock proved that the day Louis opened camp at Lakewood for the Schmeling fight. The opening took place on May 13th, 1936, and it marked Louis' 22nd birthday. Jimmy attended, along with Tony Canzoneri, the lightweight champion, and Tommy Loughran (whom he had occasion to recall very vividly). Braddock helped cut Joe's birthday cake, and was given, along with the others, a magnificent belt by Nat Fleischer, editor of the *Ring Boxing Magazine.*

"Maybe Louis is costing us plenty of money now," explained Gould. "But we're going to draw over a million dollars with that bird when we fight him. And we're going to lick him, too."

To what an extent Braddock's attitude was to endear him to the public and to react in his favor was clearly indicated near the end of Jimmy's first year as champion. If Louis got big hands when introduced, Braddock got even bigger ones as the year rounded out. There was something decidedly likeable about this big, quiet Irishman who wore his laurels so modestly and who, instead of ducking the most feared man in the heavyweight division, was ready to fight him, in his first title defense.

As summer neared, Mike Jacobs, of the Twentieth Century Club, and Madison Square Garden, quietly laid plans for their outdoor activities. Braddock was the Garden's particular property. Louis, on the other hand, was shackled to Jacobs. The canny Mike, however, put one over when, early in the year, he signed Max Schmeling to come to the United States for a fight with Louis. Recalling what had happened in the Braddock-Baer fight, Jacobs, taking no chances, also bound Schmeling for any future fights "just in case Max beat Louis."

So early in May, Schmeling and Louis pitched camps and prepared for the fight, scheduled for June 18th. (Rain eventually put the tussle over to June 19th.) Braddock, the champion, visited both camps—an unheard-of procedure. John L. Sullivan no doubt bellowed with a contemptuous rage in Valhalla when he heard the news.

The set-up, as the Louis-Schmeling fight approached, was very much akin to the set-up which preceded the Baer-Braddock tussle the year before. Schmeling was considered a "has-been." Everybody felt he had seen his best days five long years before. He was almost nine years older than Louis. He had no left hand. The slick-moving Negro, on the contrary, it seemed, had everything. He could box and he could hit. He had a left hand that fired like a piston. And his right hand was just plain murder. Yes, poor Schmeling, it was agreed, was going to a slaughter. He was being led to an electrocution. It was all so brutal. That terrible Black Menace known as Joe Louis would soon list another former world's heavyweight champion among his knockout victims. How could he help it?

But if James J. Braddock stunned the fistic world by beating Max Baer in 1935—Max Schmeling all but paralyzed it permanently by his never-to-be-forgotten knockout of Joe Louis at the Yankee Stadium on the night of June 19th, 1936. It was almost as if an earthquake had struck the Stadium. The man who had been depicted as going to his electrocution or to the gallows, hurled a crowd of some 60,000 persons into an almost maniacal frenzy as he stood off and pole-axed the 22-year-old Negro with the fiercest bombardment of solid right-hand punches thrown at any one heavyweight since Jack Dempsey had fired his famous barrage at Jess Willard in 1919. The perfect fighting machine that had been Joe Louis reeled before the impact of those murderous right-hand shots and finally tumbled down and out—yes, out—in the twelfth round, leaving everybody in the Yankee Stadium positively aghast.

Almost eight weeks had rolled by between that night of June 19th and the day this book went to press. And the "experts" (author included) were STILL bouncing on their heels, mumbling incoherently to themselves, wondering how it all happened.

James J. Braddock and Joe Gould, too, wondered how it happened—as they looked on and saw a million-dollar gate vanish into the night air. They had felt all along that Louis could be hit—but they had never figured that Schmeling would be the man to hit him. Braddock gazed with mingled emotions as the German reduced Louis to a shambles. The titleholder watched that fight from the first row in the press box. Yes, the Jerseyite who had been on relief in 1934 was journalist as well as heavyweight champion in June, 1936.

Schmeling, of course, became the new Man of the Hour as the result of his victory. But Schmeling, like Louis, was a Mike Jacobs' production and as June rolled into July, all early efforts to arrange a fight between Braddock and Schmeling were fruitless. At first, the Garden heads and Jacobs met almost daily in an effort to come to some agreement whereby the fight might be promoted. Jacobs offered either to sell his rights to Schmeling for $75,000 and a portion of the profits from the title fight—or to buy Braddock's contract from the Garden and stage the show himself. Finally, a compromise was effected. Jacobs agreed to turn Schmeling over to the Garden for the Braddock fight and the Garden in return was to transfer Tony Canzoneri, world's lightweight champion, to Jacobs for about with Barney Ross, welterweight champion and a Jacobs chattel.

It seemed as though the way for the championship bout had been paved, at last. But just when the papers were to be signed, Canzoneri's manager, Sammy Goldman, fired a monkey wrench into the proceedings. "We want a bonus of $10,000 for going over to Jacobs," said Goldman. "And we want a bigger percentage for our end. We've got something to say about being pushed around like this, too."

"Is that so?" retorted Jacobs. "Then nix."

And so on July 17th, negotiations were called off.

But this time, Braddock already had started boxing at Loch Sheldrake. He had gone to the mountains on June 6th, in fact, for several weeks of roadwork near Callicoon Center, to shift later to Loch Sheldrake where he had trained for the Baer fight. He already had assembled sparring partners. Gould had fetched Sol Flaum, George Nicholson, Tom Glynn and Bill Irby to camp to work with the champion. Maybe Gould did not know yet the man Braddock was to fight. Maybe he did not know yet for whom the champion would fight. But he was getting Braddock ready just the same.

"We'll be ready for anything," said voluble Joe. "I'm sitting tight right here in Sheldrake until the 29th of July. The Garden has to name a challenger by that time. That challenger has to be Schmeling. Doesn't the New York Commission say so? And it is up to the Garden to get him. If they can't—that's their hard luck. I can't help it if Jacobs has Schmeling under contract—can I?"

So, while Braddock trained and Gould golfed the fate of the fight rose and fell on 49th street, New York. Then, within a few days things happened.

On Monday, July 20th, Mike Jacobs announced that Joe Louis would fight his "comeback" bout against Jack Sharkey, of Boston, at the Yankee Stadium, on August 18th. On Tuesday, July 21st, Schmeling (who had returned to Germany a few days after knocking Louis out) cabled to the New York Commission his formal challenge for a shot at the heavyweight title. At the meeting of the commission that morning, Jacobs appeared on Schmeling's behalf to post a check of $5,000 as a guarantee of the German's good faith. Accompanying Jacobs was Joe Gould, who had rushed down from Sheldrake the night before.

Also present at this meeting of the solons was Jimmy Johnston of the Garden. Johnston hinted that the Garden might name Baer as Braddock's foe when July 29th rolled around and asked what would happen in case the Garden insisted on holding Braddock to his contract and Jacobs did likewise as far as Schmeling was concerned.

"The promoter who comes to the commission with the contracts of both fighters gets the show," retorted General Phelan.

All hands left the commission meeting planning to sit tight until July 29th, on which date the Garden had to name Braddock's foe. Informed very brusquely by Commissioner Bill Brown that Baer "had no status as a challenger in New York State," Johnston indicated that he was thinking seriously of John Henry Lewis as the Garden's nominee to fight Braddock.

But very suddenly, after a series of added conferences between Jacobs and Stanton Griffis, chairman of the Garden Board of Directors, the news broke that an agreement had been reached at last and that the Garden and Jacobs would jointly promote the championship fight.

Apparently, the Garden had heard from Colonel John R. Kilpatrick, its president, who had gone to Germany to find out Schmeling's exact status insofar as his contracts with Jacobs were concerned.

So, after a flood of varying rumors had swept up and down Tin Ear Alley over the weekend of July 25th, the definite announcement was made on Monday, July 27th, that the fight had been closed—and that it would be staged the last week in September at the Garden's Long Island City Bowl where Braddock had won the title the year before.

Braddock celebrated the news by roaring through seven rounds of boxing at Loch Sheldrake that afternoon and Gould celebrated by roaring angrily to the newspapers that "he had not signed as yet" and that he was not at all satisfied with the 42½ percent cut to be given the champion by the Garden for defending his title against Schmeling. (In the past, champions usually congratulated themselves when they got as high as 37½ percent.)

"I am asking 47½ percent for Braddock's end," he thundered.

"Why don't you ask for 50 percent?" a reporter asked.

"I'll be frank with you," replied Gould slyly. "I don't think I can get it."

Appendix

RECORDS OF PREVIOUS HEAVY WEIGHT CHAMPIONSHIP FIGHTS

Year	Winner	Loser	Site	Rounds
1882	John L. Sullivan	Paddy Ryan	Mississippi City, MS	9 K.
1889	John L. Sullivan	Jake Kilrain	Richburg, MS	75 D.
1892	James J. Corbett	John L. Sullivan.	New Orleans, LA	21 K.
1894	James J. Corbett	Charles Mitchell	Jacksonville, FL	3 K.
1897	Bob Fitzsimmons	James J. Corbett	Carson City, NV	14 K.
1899	James J. Jeffries	Bob Fitzsimmons	Coney Island, NY	11 K.
1899	James J. Jeffries	Tom Sharkey	Coney Island, NY	25 D.
1902	James J. Jeffries	Bob Fitzsimmons	San Francisco, CA	8 K.
1903	James J. Jeffries	James J. Corbett	San Francisco, CA	10 K.
1904	James J. Jeffries	Jack Munroe	San Francisco, CA	2 K.
1905	James J. Jeffries	Retired		
190$	Marvin Hart(x)	Jack Root	Reno, NV	12 K.
1906	Tommy Burns	Marvin Hart	Los Angeles, CA	20 D.
1907	Tommy Burns	Jack O'Brien	Los Angeles, CA	20 D.
1907	Tommy Burns	Bill Squires	Colma, CA	1 K.
1908	Jack Johnson	Tommy Burns	Sydney, Australia	14 K.
1909	Jack Johnson	Stanley Ketchel	Colma, CA	12 K.
1910	Jack Johnson	James J. Jeffries	Reno, NV	15 K.
1912	Jack Johnson	Jim Flynn	Las Vegas, NV	9 S.
1914	Jack Johnson	Frank Moran	Paris, France	20 D.
1915	Jess Willard	Jack Johnson	Havana, Cuba	26 K.
1916	Jess Willard	Frank Moran	New York, NY	10 N.D.
1919	Jack Dempsey	Jess Willard	Toledo, OH	3 K.
1920	Jack Dempsey	Billy Miske	Benton Harbor, MI	3 K.
1920	Jack Dempsey	Bill Brennan.	New York, NY	12 K.
1921	Jack Dempsey	George Carpentier	Jersey City, NJ	4 K.
192$	Jack Dempsey	Tommy Gibbons	Shelby, MT	15 D.
1923	Jack Dempsey	Louis Firpo	New York, NY	2 K.
1926	Gene Tunney	Jack Dempsey	Philadelphia, PA	10 D.
1927	Gene Tunney	Jack Dempsey	Chicago, IL	10 D.
1928	Gene Tunney	Tom Heeney.	New York, NY	11 K.
1923	Gene Tunney	Retired		
1930	Max Schmeling(x)	Jack Sharkey	New York, NY	4 F.
1931	Max Schmeling	Bill Stribling	Cleveland, OH	15 K.
1932	Jack Sharkey	Max Schmeling	Long Island City, NY	15 D.
1933	Primo Carnera	Jack Sharkey	Long Island, City, NY	6 K.
1933	Primo Carnera	Paulino Uzcudun	Rome, Italy	15 D.
1934	Primo Carnera	Tommy Loughran	Miami, FL	15 D.

1934	Max Baer	Primo Carnera	Long Island City, NY	11 T.K.
1934	Max Baer	King Levinsky	Chicago, IL	2 K.
1935	Max Baer	Eddie Simms	Cleveland, OH	4 N.D.
1935	James J. Braddock	Max Baer	Long Island City, NY	15 D.

(x) Recognized as champion. (K.) Knockout. (T.K.) Technical Knockout. (D.) Decision. (S.) Stopped by police. (N.D.) No official decision. (F.) Foul.

COMPARATIVE WEIGHTS, ETC. OF QUEENSBERRY CHAMPIONS AT TIME THEY WON HEAVYWEIGHT TITLE

	Age at which title was won	Weight	Height
James J. Braddock	29 (1935)	191¾	6 ft. 3 in.
Max Adelbert Baer	25 (1934)	208	6 ft. 2½ in.
Primo Carnera	24 (1933)	260½	6 ft. 7 in.
Jack Sharkey	29 (1932)	205	6 ft.
Max Schmeling	24 (1930)*	187	6 ft. 1 in.
Gene Tunney	28 (1926)	185½	6 ft. 1½ in.
Jack Dempsey	23 (1919)	187	6 ft. 1 in.
Jess Willard	31 (1915)	237	6 ft. 6 in.
Jack Johnson	30 (1908)	208	6 ft. 1 in.
Tommy Burns	25 (1906)	175	6 ft. 7 in.
Marvin Hart	29 (1905)**	190	5 ft. 11 in.
James J. Jeffries	24 (1899)	220	6 ft. 1½ in.
Robert Fitzsimmons	34 (1897)	156½	5 ft. 11 in.
James J. Corbett	26 (1892)	186	6 ft. 1 in.
John L. Sullivan	24 (1882)***	190	5 ft. 10½ in.

*For first fight with Jack Sharkey which Schmeling won on a foul in fourth round and as a result of which he was recognized by N.Y. Boxing Commission as successor of Gene Tunney, who retired undefeated in 1928.

**For fight with Jack Root, which Hart won and which earned him recognition as the successor to James J. Jeffries, who had announced his retirement from the ring in 1905 after three years of idleness, due to a lack of challengers.

***Figures for Sullivan are for his fight with Paddy Ryan for the London Prize Ring title.

FISTIC RECORD OF JAMES J. BRADDOCK

1935	June 13	Max Baer	Won Decision	15 Rds.	Long Island City
	March 22	Art Lasky	Won Decision	15 Rds.	New York
1934	Nov. 16	John Henry Lewis	Won Decision	10 Rds.	New York
	June 14	Corn Griffin	Won by Kayo	3 Rds.	Long Island City
1933	Sept. 25	Abe Feldman	No Contest (broke hand)	6 Rds.	Mount Vernon
	July 21	Chester Matan	Won Decision	10 Rds.	West New York
	June 21	Less Kennedy	Won Decision	10 Rds.	Jersey City
	May 19	Al Stillman	Lost Decision	10 Rds.	St. Louis
	April 5	Martin Levandowski	Lost Decision	10 Rds.	St. Louis
	March 21	Al Stillman	Won by T.K.O.	10 Rds.	St. Louis
	March 1	Al Ettore	Lost (no contest)	4 Rds.	Philadelphia
	Jan. 20	Hans Birkie	Lost Decision	10 Rds.	New York
	Jan. 13	Martin Levandowski	Won Decision	10 Rds.	Chicago
1932	Nov. 9	Lou Scozza	Lost by T.K.O.	6 Rds.	San Francisco
	Oct. 21	Tom Patrick	Lost Decision	10 Rds.	Hollywood
	Sept. 21	John Henry Lewis	Lost Decision	10 Rds.	San Francisco
	Sept. 30	Dynamite Jackson	Won Decision	10 Rds.	San Diego
	July 25	Tony Shucco	Lost Decision	8 Rds.	New York
	June 21	Vincent Parille	Won Decision	5 Rds.	New York
	May 13	Charley Retzlaff	Lost Decision	10 Rds.	Boston
	March 18	Baxter Calmes	Lost Decision	10 Rds.	Chicago
1931	Dec. 4	Al Gainer	Lost Decision	10 Rds.	New Haven
	Nov. 10	Maxie Rosenbloom	No Contest	2 Rds.	Minneapolis
	Oct. 9	Joe Sekyra	Lost Decision	10 Rds.	New York
	Sept. 3	Andy Mitchell	Draw	10 Rds.	Detroit
	March 30	Jack Kelly	Won Decision	10 Rds.	Waterbury
	March 5	Jack Roper	Won by K.O.	1 Rd.	Miami
	Jan. 23	Ernie Schaaf	Lost Decision	10 Rds.	New York
1930	Sept. 19	Phil Mercurio	Won by K.O.	2 Rds.	Boston
	Aug. 12	Babe Hunt	Lost Decision	10 Rds.	Boston
	July 2	Joe Monte	Won Decision	10 Rds.	Boston
	June 5	Harold Mays	Won Decision	10 Rds.	West New York
	April 7	Billy Jones	Lost Decision	10 Rds.	Philadelphia
	Jan. 17	Leo Lomski	Lost Decision	10 Rds.	Chicago
1929	Dec. 7	Jake Warren	Won by K.O.	2 Rds.	New York
	Nov. 15	Max Rosenbloom	Lost Decision	10 Rds.	New York

	Aug. 27	Yale Okun	Lost Decision	10 Rds.	Los Angeles
	July 18	Tommy Loughran	Lost Decision	15 Rds.	New York
	April 22	Eddie Benson	Won by K.O.	1 Rd.	Buffalo
	March 11	Jimmy Slattery	Won by K.O.	9 Rds.	New York
	Feb. 4	George Gemas	Won by K.O.	1 Rd.	Newark
	Jan. 18	Leo Lomski	Lost Decision	10 Rds.	New York
1928	Nov. 30	Tuffy Griffiths	Won by K.O.	2 Rds.	New York
	Oct. 17	Pete Latzo	Won Decision	10 Rds.	Newark
	Aug. 8	Joe Sekyra	Lost Decision	10 Rds.	New York
	July 25	Nando Tassi	Draw	10 Rds.	New York
	June 27	Bill Vidabeck	No Decision	10Rds.	West New York
	June 7	Joe Monte	Draw	10Rds.	New York
	May 16	Jimmy Francis	Won Decision	10Rds.	West New York
	May 7	Jack Darnell	Won by K.O.	4 Rds.	Jersey City
	Jan. 6	Paull Swiderski	Won Decision	10 Rds.	New York

1927 KNOCKOUTS—Johnny Alberts, 3; George LaRocco, 1; Tom McKiernan, 2; Frankie Lennon, 3; Stanly Simmons, 1.
NO DECISIONS—Doc Conrad, 6; Paul Cavalier, 10; Germany Heller, 10; Jimmy Francis, 10; Jack Stone, 10; Jimmy Francis, 10.
WON—Vic McLoughlin, 10; Nick Fadil, 6; Lew Barba, 6; George LaRocco, 6.
DRAW—George LaRocco, 6; Joe Monte, 10.

1926 KNOCKOUTS—Leo Dobson, 2; Walter Westman, 3; George Deschner, 2; Jim Pearson, 2; Gene Travers, 1; Mike Rock, 1; Ray Kennedy, 1; Phil Weisberger, 1; Carmine Caggiano, 1; Jack O'Day, 1; Willie Daly, 1.
NO DECISIONS—Al Settle, 6; Joe Hudson, 6; Al Settle, 6.
WON—Lew Barba, 6.
(Dates for most of his fights in 1926 and 1927 will be found in early chapters of the book.)

(Amateur Record)
Had 45 fights as an amateur in 1924, 1925 and 1926, winning 30 by knockout. Won New Jersey State Amateur Light-Heavyweight and Heavyweight Championship in 1925 and 1926.

Fought his first fight in a ring November 27th, 1923, under the name of Jimmy Ryan, at Moose Hall, Grantwood, N.J. and lost newspaper decision to Tommy Hummell.

Printed in Great Britain
by Amazon

15415570R00129